Nintendo ∨ Genesis ∨ TurboGrafx-16

™

D0754023

From the Editors of GamePro Magazine
The Unauthorized Nintendo, Genesis, & TurboGrafx-16 Tips Guide

IDG BOOKS WORLDWIDE

AN INTERNATIONAL DATA GROUP COMPANY

To Patrick Ferrell
Thanks – Your energy, enthusiasm, and humor
are a source of inspiration for us all!

(And to Bill Murphy, without whom this book
would not have been possible.)

Written and edited: LeeAnne McDermott, Michael Meyers, and Wesley Nihei.
Production and Production Coordination: Lynne Kavish
Art Direction and Design: Michael Kavish
Cover Illustration: John Mattos
Interior Illustration: Francis Mao
Technical Assistance: David Winstead

ISBN #1-878058-00-2

10 9 8 7 6 5 4 3 2 1

Table of Contents

Table of Contents

Introduction

Welcome to GamePro's Hot Tips: Sports Games. Here at GamePro we play video games for a living and we know what kinds of information help us to improve our gameplay. But when we sat down to write this book we still asked ourselves, "What does the serious video game sports fan want in a game tips book?" To discover the answer we took a look at what you, the experts, had to say – we opened our mail! Based on your letters and phone calls we know that what matters to you are winning techniques to help you improve your scores and make you a better player. So that's what we've packed this book with – the hottest tips, tactics, and passwords, or S.W.A.T. (Special Weapons and Tactics) from GamePro Magazine, for the most popular sports games available.

And there's more! You'll also find a brief description of each game as well as color screen shots to show you how the game looks. We've also tagged a Reader's Choice icon to 20 games that were picked as favorites by GamePro readers everywhere. Near the end of the book you'll find a section on up and coming sports titles. Finally, just for you, there's a stack of discount coupons for your favorite game titles in the back of the book.

Okay, sports fans, enough talk. On your mark, get set, GO!

P.S. Don't forget – as always when we say "GamePro" we mean you! Send us your tips and tactics and you might find yourself in the next book, or an issue of GamePro Magazine. Send mail to GamePro, P.O. Box 3329, Redwood City, CA 94064. And don't forget to check out our companion book, GamePro Hot Tips: Adventure Games. It's packed with great tips and tactics, too!

Copyrights

Bad News Baseball is a TM of Tecmo, Ltd., ©1990 Tecmo Ltd. Bases Loaded is a TM of Jaleco USA, Inc., ©1989 Jaleco USA, Inc. Bases Loaded II: The Second Season is a TM of Jaleco USA, Inc., ©1989 Jaleco USA, Inc. Baseball Simulator 1.000 is a TM of Culture Brain USA, Inc., ©1989 Culture Brain USA, Inc. Baseball Stars is a TM of SNK Corporation of America, ©1989 SNK Corporation of America. Dusty Diamond's All-Star Softball is a TM of Broderbund Software, Inc., ©1989 Tokyo Shoseki, ©1990 Broderbund Software, Inc. Little League Baseball Championship Series is a TM of SNK Corporation of America, ©1990 SNK Corporation of America. RBI is a TM of Atari Games Corporation, ©1986, 1987 NAMCO, ©1987 Atari Games Corporation. RBI 2 is a TM of Atari Games Corporation, ©1990 Tengen, Inc. Tommy Lasorda Baseball is a TM of Sega of America, Inc., ©1989 Sega of America, Inc. World Class Baseball is a TM of NEC Home Electronics (U.S.A.) Inc., ©1989 NEC Home Electronics (U.S.A.) Inc. Cyberball is a TM of Atari Games Corporation, ©1990 Tengen, Inc., ©1990 Sega of America, Inc. John Elway's Quarterback is a TM of The Leland Corporation, ©1988 Tradewest, Inc. NFL Football game pak is a TM of LJN Toys, Ltd., ©1988 LJN Toys, Ltd. NFL and the NFL shield are trademarks of the National Football League. Tecmo Bowl is a TM of Tecmo, Inc., ©1989 Tecmo, Inc. NFL Players Association ©1988 NFLPA ©MSA. T.V. Sports Football is a TM of Cinemaware Corp, ©1990 Cinemaware Corp. All Pro Basketball is a TM of Vic Tokai, Inc., ©1989 Vic Tokai, Inc. Double Dribble is a TM of Konami Industry Co., Ltd., ©1987 Konami Industry Co., Ltd. Hoops is a TM of Jaleco USA, Inc., ©1989 Jaleco USA, Inc. One on One is a TM of Electronic Arts, ©1988 Electronic Arts, ©1989 Milton Bradley Company. Magic Johnson's Fast Break is a TM of Virgin Mastertronic, International, ©1990 Virgin Mastertronic International. Pat Riley's Basketball is a TM of Sega of America, Inc., ©1990 Sega of America, Inc. Takin' It To The Hoop is a TM of Hudson Soft, ©1989 AICOM Corporation, ©1990 NEC Technologies, Inc. Goal is a TM of Jaleco USA, Inc., ©1989 Jaleco USA, Inc. World Championship Soccer is a TM of Sega of America, Inc., ©1989 Sega of America, Inc. Al Unser's Turbo Racing is a TM of Data East USA, Inc., ©1988 Data East USA, Inc. Bigfoot and 4x4x4 are trademarks of Bigfoot 4x4x4 Inc. Gamepak ©1989 Acclaim Entertainment, Inc. Final Lap Twin is a TM of NAMCO, Ltd., ©1990 NEC Technologies, Inc. Michael Andretti's World GP is a TM of American Sammy Corporation, ©1990 American Sammy Corporation. Moto Roader is a TM of NEC Home Technologies (USA) Inc., ©1989 NEC Home Technologies (USA) Inc. Rad Racer is a TM of Nintendo of America, Inc., ©1987 Square, ©1987 Nintendo of America, Inc. Rad Racer II is a TM of Square, ©1990 Square. RC Pro Am is a TM of Nintendo of America, Inc., ©1987 Rare Limited. Super Hang On is a TM of Sega of America, Inc., ©1989 Sega of America, Inc. Ivan "Ironman" Stewart's Super Off Road is a TM of Tradewest, Inc., ©1989 Tradewest, Inc. Super Sprint is a ® of Atari Games Corporation, ©1986 Atari Games Corporation, ©1989 Tengen, Inc. Victory Run is a TM of NEC Home Technologies (USA) Inc., ©1989 NEC Home Technologies (USA) Inc. Racket Attack is a TM of Jaleco USA, Inc., ©1988 Jaleco USA, Inc. Top Players Tennis is a TM of Asmik Corporation of America, ©1989 Asmik Corporation of America. World Court Tennis is a TM of NAMCO, Ltd., ©1987, 1989 NAMCO, Ltd., ©1989 NEC Home Electronics (USA) Ltd. Arnold Palmer Tournament Golf is a TM of Sega of America, Inc., ©1989 Sega of America, Inc. Bandai Golf – Challenge Pebble Beach is a TM of Bandai America, Inc., ©1988 Bandai America, Inc. Jack Nicklaus's Greatest 18 Holes of Major Championship Golf is produced in association with Jack Nicklaus Productions, Inc. The Golden Bear Symbol and TM of Golden Bear International, Inc. Licensed from Accolade Inc., ©1989 Accolade Inc., ©1989 Konami Ultra Inc. Lee Trevino's Fighting Golf is a TM of SNK Electronics Corporation, ©1988 SNK Electronics Corporation. Power Golf is a TM of Hudson Soft, ©1989 Hudson Soft and NEC Home Electronics (USA) Inc. Budokan is a TM of Electronic Arts, ©1990 Electronic Arts. Mike Tyson's Punch-Out is a ® of Nintendo of America, Inc., ©1987 Nintendo of America, Inc. Tecmo World Wrestling is a TM is Tecmo, Ltd., ©1990 Tecmo, Ltd. WCW and World Championship Wrestling are service marks and registered trademarks of World Championship Wrestling, Inc., and are licensed to FCI. Game pak ©1989 FCI/Pony Canyon, Inc. and Nihon Bussan Co., Ltd. WWF and Wrestlemania are registered trademarks of TitanSports, Inc., Hulk Hogan is a TM of the Marvel Comics Group, licensed to TitanSport, Inc. All other distinctive names and character likenesses are trademarks of TitanSports. ©1988 TitanSports. Game pak ©1988 Acclaim Entertainment, Inc. 720 Degrees is a TM of Atari Games Corporation, ©1986 Atari Games Corporation, ©1986 Tengen, Inc. Skate or Die is a ® of Electronic Arts, ©1988 Ultra Software Corporation. Town and Country is a ® of Town and Country Surf Shop, Ltd., ©1987 Town and Country Surf Shop, Ltd. Game Pak, ©1987 LJN Toys, Ltd. California Games is a TM of Epyx, Inc., ©1987 Epyx, Inc. MB and Milton Bradley are trademarks of Milton Bradley Company. Game pak ©1988 Milton Bradley Company. Track and Field is a TM of Konami Industry Co., Ltd., ©1987 Konami, Inc. Track and Field II is a TM of Konami Industry Co., Ltd., ©1988 Konami, Inc. World Games is a ® of Epyx, Inc. ©1986 Epyx, Inc., ©1988 Milton Bradley Company. Blades of Steel is a TM of Konami Industry Co., Ltd. ©1988 Konami Industry Co., Ltd. Black Bass Fishing is a TM of HOT-B USA, Inc., ©1989 HOT-B USA, Inc. Championship Bowling is a TM of Romstar Incorporated, ©1989 Romstar Incorporated. Heavy Shreddin' is a TM of Imagineering, Inc., ©1989 Imagineering, Inc. Kings of the Beach is a TM of Electronic Arts, ©1989 Ultra Software Corporation. Super Dodge Ball is a TM of Technos Japan Corporation, ©1988 Technos Japan Corporation. Toobin' is a ® of Atari Games Corporation, ©1989 Tengen, Inc. Arch Rivals is a TM of Rare Coin-It, Inc., ©1989 Rare Coin-It, Inc. Battle Royale is a TM of Incredible Technologies, Inc., ©1990 NEC Home Technologies (USA) Inc. Hard Drivin' is a TM of Atari Games Corporation, ©1989 Atari Games Corporation. James Buster Douglas Knock-Out Boxing is a TM of Sega of America, Inc., ©1990 Sega of America, Inc. Joe Montana Football is a TM of Sega of America, Inc., ©1990 Sega of America, Inc. Matchbox Racers is a TM of Matchbox International, ©1990 Matchbox International. Mike Ditka's Big Play Football ©1989, 1990 Pony Canyon, Inc/Natsume. All other materials ©1990, Accolade, Inc. All rights reserved. Mondu's Fight Palace is a TM of Activision, ©1990 Activision. Super Monaco GP is a TM of Sega of America, ©1990 Sega of America, Inc. Super Volleyball is a TM of NEC Home Technologies (USA) Inc., ©1990 Video System. T.V. Sports Basketball is a TM of NEC Home Technologies (USA) Inc., ©1990 Cinemaware Corporation. Ultimate Basketball is a TM of American Sammy Corporation, ©1990 American Sammy Corporation. War on Wheels is a TM of Jaleco USA, Inc., ©1990 Jaleco USA, Inc. World Trophy Soccer is a TM of Arcadia, ©1990 INTV Corporation., licensed from Arcadia Systems. Zany Golf is a TM of Bullfrog Software and Electronic Arts, ©1990 Electronic Arts.

By Tecmo
One or Two Players (simultaneous)

Welcome to the world of Bad News Baseball, a place where rabbits serve as umpires, homeruns escape the earth's atmosphere, and batters are knocked unconscious when they make an out.

Bad News Baseball is a Japanese import for a younger audience. The cart has two leagues – the Ultra and the Super leagues – with 12 teams that represent major league cities without using real team or player names. There are several play modes to choose from at the start of the game. You can play a One Player tournament versus the computer: pick a team and play against every other team once. Or, you can play a three-game series against a friend. There's also an all-star mode, which enables you to build a 23-player team from the rosters of the Ultra or Super league. And if you just want to watch a game, there's a spectator mode.

As in other baseball games, pitching and defense are as important as hitting. Pitchers have the basic array of pitches – fastballs, curves, sliders, and changeups. Effectiveness depends on the ERA. Batting is similar to that of RBI Baseball, Major League Baseball, and other "home plate view" games. You don't have to worry about the height of the pitch, just whether or not it's over the plate. In the infield and outfield it's up to you whether your team will make a double play or an error.

Bad News Baseball is a hilarious alternative for baseball video gamers, especially those who take the game too seriously. After all, how mad can you get when you get a bad call from a rabbit, especially one that hangs out in hot tubs!

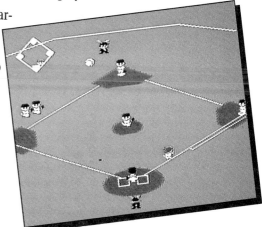

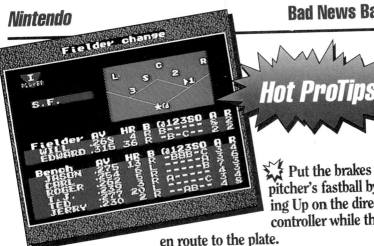

Put the brakes on your pitcher's fastball by pushing Up on the directional controller while the ball is en route to the plate.

Fielders are rated A, B, and C at one or more positions. If possible, try to have A-rated players at every position. "A" players can do the extras such as jump for balls over their heads or dive for balls out of reach. "B" players have average skills and C players have limited range.

For some really adventuresome defense, try placing a player at a position for which he isn't rated!

The running game is a key ingredient in a successful game of Bad News Baseball. Runners are rated from 1 to 8, with 8 being the fastest. A runner with an 8 rating can usually beat out a bunt for a hit, then steal second and third unchallenged.

In the One-Player Pennant Mode you can make the rabbit in the hot tub make "bubbles" by pressing Button B on the controller once while on the password screen.

Change all of the teams to girls teams – including the special super-powered team and special players – by doing the following: during the title screen press diagonally Down and Left on Controller One, while simultaneously pressing Up on Controller Two. While holding both control pads press Reset on your NES. Now, while still holding the control pads, press the Start button on Controller One. This changes all the teams to girls teams! You'll know it's worked if the baseball icon changes to a heart. The Texas team becomes a super-star team. There will also be a few super superstars on some of the other teams.

By Jaleco
One or Two Players (simultaneous)

Admit it, it's easy to be a back-seat manager from the safety of your living room couch. Hey coach wanna-be's, it's your chance to put your money where your mouth is. Jaleco's original Bases Loaded cart puts you in the dugout, at the plate, on the mound, in center field, and just about everywhere except in the stands.

You're in for the long haul in this cart. Choose from two modes of play. In the Pennant Mode you're up against the computer in a 132-game season. You can also go head-to-head against a friend in a one-game series.

Pick your winning team from 12 different squads. Each team has a roster of 30 players, including 12 pitchers. Every team is different, with every player having his own ERA and unique personality, including being left- or right-handed. The starting lineup for each game is preset – except that you get to choose your pitcher. But you can substitute throughout each nine-inning game, so you'll have plenty of chances to exercise your managerial brilliance.

Since you're a player manager you'll have to do more than simply know your team inside and out in order to use them effectively. You'll also have to be an all-star on the field! After all you're going to pitch, field, and bat all by yourself! Throw a strike, hit a Grand Slam, make a spectacular diving catch – it's all up to you!

Additional realistic touches include the inspirational cheering of the crowd and the clear voices of the umpires making their calls. Bases Loaded is top baseball simulation. Now get out there and play ball!

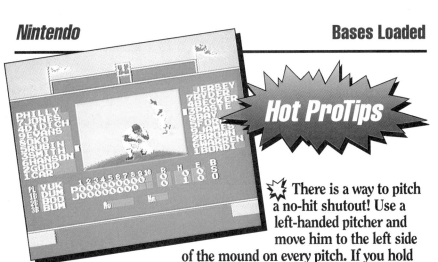

☆ There is a way to pitch a no-hit shutout! Use a left-handed pitcher and move him to the left side of the mound on every pitch. If you hold Down on the controller while the pitcher throws his pitch, the computer won't swing at the ball. You can keep this up until about halfway through the fifth inning. Then, bring in a lefty relief pitcher and continue to hold Down while pitching.

☆ Some pitchers will occasionally throw bean balls! Here's what you have to do to make the batter mad enough to cause him to attack your pitcher (and get ejected from the game). 1) It must be AFTER the third inning. 2) It must be the number three or four hitter in the lineup. This strategy is very effective in a close ballgame. Since the number three or four batter is often the player who carries the offense for a team, having him replaced with a bench player after he has been ejected makes things a lot easier on your pitcher for the remainder of the game.

☆ To keep your players from being ejected during a brawl when they charge the mound after being beaned try the following: When your player gets hit with a pitch, continuously press Button B until the next batter comes to the plate. Your fighting player will stay in the game!

☆ Yes, it is possible to bring in a Pinch Hitter or Reliever if you're Player #2! Here's what to do: Player #1's controller is the only controller capable of calling "time-out." After time has been called by Player #1, Player #2 should press his A Button. Player #2's selection screen will appear and he can proceed as normal.

☆ Up on the scoreboard you may have noticed that the words "Yuk, Dum, Boo, Bum" appear in the lower left corner. Is this some secret Egyptian hieroglyphic? Perhaps a secret code that would bring

Link to the plate for your team? In actuality, "Yuk" is the name of the homeplate umpire. "Dum" is the first base ump. "Boo" is the second base ump. And "Bum" is the third base ump! And you thought "Who", "What", and "I Don't Know" were dumb names!

 Here's a quick overview of some of the best Bases Loaded teams:

PHILLY: A well-balanced team. Good hitting and pitching. Gantos is the #1 starter – he has a great fastball and the best vertical curve. Oko is ranked in the top ten for average and homeruns. Their leadoff hitter, Jones, has great speed and is an excellent basestealer.

DC: Very good power, average pitching. Fendy finished 2nd in homeruns and 5th in batting average. Best basestealer is Gomez. The #1 starter for DC is Morgan. He has the best velocity on his fastball and the best movement on his curves.

BOSTON: This offensive machine is the top homerun-hitting squad in Bases Loaded. The entire front half of the batting order could pop a dinger at any given at-bat. Freida is second on the batting average list and third on the homerun list. Lots of speed sitting on the Boston bench including the fastest player in Bases Loaded: Uma. Pitching is solid but not spectacular.

JERSEY: Here lives the best baseball player to ever step into a Bases Loaded contest. His name is Paste, and he carries an average team on his back. He is the leader in batting average and homeruns. He makes opposing pitchers tremble in fear. The rest of the Jersey team is ho-hum. The Jersey pitching staff is below average. Well...you can't have everything!

 Every Bases Loaded team has a staff of 12 pitchers. Every staff is a mixture of starters and relievers. Your starters have stamina, and ideally should be effective for six to eight innings. Relievers have much less stamina and usually aren't effective more than a couple of innings. But how do you know who is a starter and who is a reliever? Up till now it's been guesswork, but no longer with our starting pitcher list! When there is a clear-cut #1 starter on the team, a #1 appears in brackets next to the name.

PHILLY: Gantos, Morris, Stone, and Ellis
DC: Knapp, Sether, Morgan, Fern, and Thomas
BOSTON: Fine (#1), Birdie, Pacos, Creene, Rosa, Bakko, and Ballou

JERSEY: Valez, Greco, Westin, Scott, Less, and Rose
KANSAS: Mills, Black, Carter (#1), Rick, and Platt
N.Y.: Hodges, Fillo, King, Cora, Flore, and Howe
MIAMI: Bonds, Shard, Jowel, Irving (#1), Jarvis, Nudor, and Olson
HAWAII: Cuomo, Cook, Ford, York, and Tamino
UTAH: Stava, Tillis (#1), Bella, Murray, Lund, and Miller
L.A.: Moral, Thomsy (#1), Smithe, Jonas, and Bailey (#1)
TEXAS: Kramer, Major, Tutor, Newton, Reilly (#1), and Sax
OMAHA: Anders, Hunt, Watts, Gibbs, Miles, Foot, and Hallas

Passwords

The following are passwords to the last game (the pennant clincher) of
Bases Loaded for any team:

Boston:	LFBDJHE	Kansas:	PNCBNHD
New York:	PFDAJHH	Utah:	LNBCJPD
Philly:	LFDBJHE	Hawaii:	LNADJPD
D.C.:	PFACNHK	Omaha:	LNDAJPD
Jersey:	LFADNHH	Texas:	LNCBJPD
Miami:	PFCANHK	LA:	PFBCNPD

Try the following password for fun:

JAELECO

By Jaleco
One or Two Players (simultaneous)

The roar of the crowd, the crack of the bat, the umpire yelling "safe", the smell of roasted peanuts – deja vu? Nope, it's Jaleco's new and improved Bases Loaded II – the Second Season!

In this version of Bases Loaded you coach your team through a 130-game season in either an Eastern or Western division of a professional baseball league. Win the pennant and you're off to the World Series! You can also play head-to-head with a friend.

Choose from six teams in each division, including the likes of Jersey and Philly. Once you take your place in the dugout you're the manager, juggling your own lineup and batting order. You'll also have to be somewhat of a psychologist as you learn to interpret the Player Performance Ratings. This unique feature of Bases Loaded II rates each player in three different categories: physical, sensitivity, and intellectual.

Each rating is like a biorhythm, going up and down, just as in real life! And that's what it's all about. The Player Performance Ratings simulate what players really go through – streaks and slumps! It's up to you to decide when to bench your players for a couple of games until they're back on track.

Once the action starts you control pitching, hitting, and fielding just as in Bases Loaded. Realistic action and the Players Performance Ratings combine to make Bases Loaded II one of the most exciting baseball simulations available for the NES.

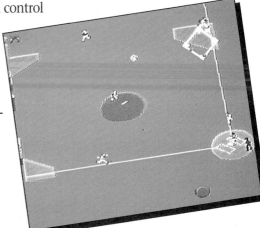

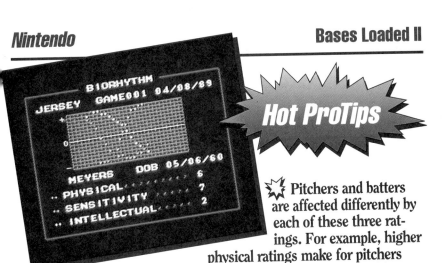

🌟 Pitchers and batters are affected differently by each of these three ratings. For example, higher physical ratings make for pitchers who throw the ball faster with greater control, and batters who get hits. A low sensitivity rating for a pitcher might indicate he isn't really up emotionally for the game. For a batter it might indicate that his powerhitting ability is going to be off in the next game.

🌟 You'll find that two teams have somewhat familiar names. The ballplayers on the D.C. Ringers team have political names. From Hall and North to a pitching bullpen packed with the likes of Regan, Ford, Nixon, Bush, and Quail, it's one odd team. The Los Angeles team is made up of Hollywood's big names from today and yesterday – from Cosby to Carson to Pacino.

🌟 Jersey is one of the most powerful teams in the game and it's really the Jaleco team, with several Jaleco employees on the squad. This team has the most speed on the basepaths of any team in the game. Weir is a prolific base stealer (make sure to move him into the lead-off spot before starting a game). Jersey also has a top-notch pitching staff.

🌟 Power and pitching is what Boston is all about. Deaff, Teylan, and Storm are the most dangerous three, four, and five hitters in the league. This Boston team needs to hit a lot of homers since they have no running speed. Juarez is one of the top starting pitchers in the league and Crown is an ace reliever.

🌟 New York is another team with a lot of pop. Albin, Lukas, and Palmer are an even better three, four, five combination than Boston's group. Some speed on the bench (Chiaro) and a Cy Young candidate (Ayoub).

Los Angeles has some of the best pitching in the league. Grant, Cruise, and Dreyfus are all top-notch starters. Bergen is a potential MVP powerhitter.

The following passwords start you out at 50 wins out of 50 games played with any team in Bases Loaded II:

New York:	CMDUIID	Los Angeles:	SCTLRYQ
Boston:	CNDUIIE	Kansas:	IANOXXG
Jersey:	XSQQUVO	Omaha:	ASFWGGH
Philly:	FICCJDE	Texas:	GRYYMEM
Miami:	BNGXFHF	Hawaii:	XBQQUVW
DC:	CRDUIII	Utah:	WDPPVUV

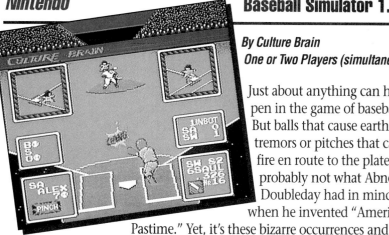

By Culture Brain
One or Two Players (simultaneous)

Just about anything can happen in the game of baseball. But balls that cause earth tremors or pitches that catch fire en route to the plate are probably not what Abner Doubleday had in mind when he invented "America's Pastime." Yet, it's these bizarre occurrences and many other special tricks that make Culture Brain's Baseball Simulator 1.000 such a kick.

In Baseball Simulator 1.000 you can choose from four different leagues; three with six preset teams each and one where you can build the teams yourself from scratch. Face the computer or challenge a friend to compete in a 5-, 30-, 60-, or 165-game season. Games take place in six stadiums, including the Dome and a stadium in outer space!

As the manager you build up your team by allocating a set bunch of points for batting average, homeruns, running speed, and fielding ability among your players. Then, you customize your pitching staff by divvying up points for ERA, speed, right and left curveballs, sinking pitches, and stamina. Your managerial responsibilities also include deciding who's right-handed and who's a lefty, and whether your pitchers throw overhand or sidearm.

If straightforward baseball is a little too mundane for you, take a turn in the Ultra League. Ultra League play enables you to give your hitters and pitchers special skills, such as the ability to pitch balls that zig zag or explode, or hit the ball into orbit.

Out of this world baseball? You bet!

You can stop the computer from using super pitching and super hitting abilities! When the computer selects a super ability, call "Time Out" and go to the Pinch Hitter or Relief Pitcher screen. Select "Cancel." Go back to the main screen, and the computer will no longer have super ability selected!

Get the most out of your starting pitchers. When you go to the bullpen you'll find your relievers don't have the stamina to go the long distance and you don't want to go through your entire pitching staff in one game.

Eliminate one of the power hitters on the other team! Bean the batter with a Fireball pitch. The batter will be removed from the game!

In Ultra Play save your Hyper Pitch for a batter with two strikes. It'll be a sure out and you won't waste your ultra points.

There is a way to make your right fielder fly through space and defy gravity! Play in the Outer Space arena. When in the field hit Start and select Shift! Move your right fielder against the fence. Hit a ball to the outfield. Your rightfielder will fly up into space!

Try giving your catcher a fielding rating of 50 or higher. Any foul tip or pop-up will automatically be caught for an out if the catcher has a high fielding rating.

A high running speed and the hitting ability, Spinner Hit, is a dangerous combination. A spinner hit gives your player enough time to circle the bases, if he has a running speed of 50 or higher.

The Ultra League ES Team starts with more ultra points than the others. Everytime you use an ultra ability it costs three ultra points, so using your ES team is smart when you're just beginning.

You can automatically move your baserunner from 1st base to 2nd base whenever you have another baserunner on 3rd base. The computer team will not throw the ball to 2nd base, or if it comes, simply take a step off 3rd base with your other baserunner. The computer will throw the ball home and you can safely advance to 2nd base.

 It is important to have a centerfielder with a high fielder rating (40 or more). The centerfielder has to cover more ground than any player on your team.

By SNK
One or Two Players (simultaneous)

Say what? You want a baseball game that lets you control absolutely everything? You want to be a player and a manager and you also want to build and manage the teams in your very own league? Impossible, right? Wrong! Baseball Stars lets you do all of that and more. Read on...

When you first sign up as a Baseball Star, you'll find that you've got more to learn than simply how to pitch, hit, and field the ball. In this game you can also create your own teams and leagues, as well as sign up new players, trade with other teams, and even send some players packing when they don't measure up.

When you take to the field, you'll find Baseball Stars also features hard-to-beat player action and great graphics. When you step up to the batter's box you can move around in the box, decide whether to swing, and even bunt the ball. As a runner on base you decide when to take an extra base, when to lead off, and when to go for the steal. When your team takes the field, you control pitching (fastball, changeup, curveball, and slider), as well as fielding (make spectacular jumping or diving catches, as well as climb the wall to snag a potential homerun)!

And, hey, if you don't like the way your team is playing, then change the batting order, put in a reliever, or move your players around on the field. After all, you're the star, and in this baseball cart you call all of the shots – from the board room to the locker room to the dugout to center field!

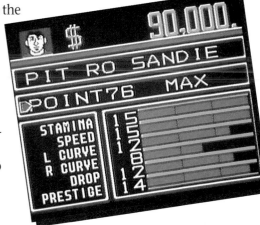

Hot ProTips

To begin with a more powerful team try the following: Starting from the upper left corner, move the cursor Down, Right, Left, Down, Down, Right, and Up with the control pad. You'll end up on the Balanced Team option. Now, press Button A and under "Enter Your Team Name" the words "WHEN ISN'T IT?" should appear. Change these words to "WHEN IT IS." and you'll be rewarded with a more powerful, well-balanced team!

To be the strongest girls team try the following pad trick. Select Make Team. On your directional controller press Down, Right, Left, Down, Down, Right, Up, Up, Down, Up, Down, and Up. Now, press Button A. "WHAT IS A WREN?" appears. Erase this and put "A BIRD." The phrase "WHEN ISN'T IT?" will appear. Erase this and put "WHEN IT IS." You're ready to go!

You can choose from several options when you build your team from scratch – should you give all of your hitters plenty of power? Make them expert fielders? Give them plenty of quickness on the bases? Here are a few hints to get your team started off on the right foot:

Like Whitey Herzog, manager of the St. Louis Cardinals, says, you build a team with speed and pitching. This is a great way to go in Baseball Stars. Make sure the top three batters in your lineup have maximum speed ratings. This allows them to beat out bunts for easy singles.

Next, give yourself two top-flight starting pitchers, one quality middle-inning reliever, and an ace stopper. With enough quality pitching to get you through nine innings at a time, and men who can steal bases at will, you'll be off to a great start.

Play against the "Lovely Ladies" several times early in the season. The Lovely Ladies are a team known for their defense. However, they aren't very good hitters, don't possess great basestealing speed, and have average pitching. Most importantly, though, they have very high prestige ratings and always attract a lot of fans to their games! Must be the cute pink uniforms they wear. Plenty of fans translates to plenty of dollars for your team when you win!

 Try to get starters who have lots of potential. Every player has a maximum of points he can accumulate. Try to trade for or hire starters who have a maximum of 70 points or higher – it leaves room for growth!

 You want to build a strong defense up the middle, just like in real baseball. Increase the defensive ratings of your Centerfielder, Shortstop, and Catcher first, and then work on the other players.

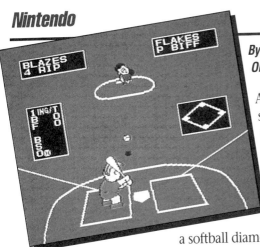

By Broderbund
One or Two Players (simultaneous)

All weekend ballplayers know softball's no joke, but that doesn't mean you can't have a little fun with it. And when you step up to the plate in this cart you'll find that these are the wackiest bunch of players to ever hit a softball diamond!

Play seven-inning fast-or slow-pitch games. In One Player mode, you face the computer in a five-game elimination tournament. Win them all, and you earn the right to challenge the awesome Amazons – All-Star Softball's all-time championship team. Of course, you and a friend can play each other in a head-to-head contest.

There are no preset ball clubs so you recruit a 10-member squad from a roster of 60 weird players. Look for players who have strong basic baseball skills such as arm strength and speed. But to win on some of the tricky fields you'll also need players with some more unusual skills – such as climbing fences, diving into water, and flying at night!

In fast pitch, you can hurl that baby in three speeds. But stay alert, baserunners steal and batters bunt. In slow pitch, you can lob the ball short or long. You can also make your pitches curve left or right.

Fielding the ball takes practice, but your guys can also dive for hard grounders and leap up to snare line shots! For quick double plays, infielders can tag a base then throw the ball.

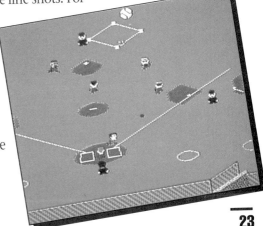

With six softball fields to choose from, including the Sandlot, the Cliff, and a Professional field, there's some great action! Get ready to take yourself out to the softball park!

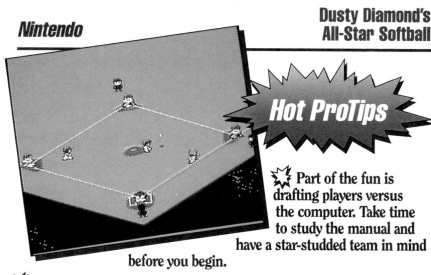

Hot ProTips

⭐ Part of the fun is drafting players versus the computer. Take time to study the manual and have a star-studded team in mind before you begin.

⭐ When you pitch against your buddy, try to fool him by quickly sliding your pitcher around on the mound with the Left and Right keys up to the instant before you make your pitch.

⭐ Use Left and Right to move your pitcher around on the mound to vary the location of his pitches. Stay in one spot and the batters tee-off on you.

⭐ Pitchers tire, so sub frequently. Try to have two good pitchers on your team. Some players don't have pitching ratings, but they aren't bad hurlers – experiment.

⭐ When you play the computer fast pitch, use pitches to set up the batters. A tight inside pitch brushes the batter back, and he'll stay back until after the next pitch. So toss a quick pitch to the outside corner for a strike.

⭐ Just as in some softball leagues, hit a foul ball after two strikes and you're out.

⭐ When you're at bat take a few cuts at the plate to see where the thick part of the bat creates a power zone. You'll have to move if the pitcher repositions himself.

⭐ Consider moving your batter around in the batter's box after the pitch to hit the ball with the sweet spot on the bat.

⭐ If you have men on base and the batter hits a fly ball, your runners take off automatically. If the fielder catches the ball, you must make the lead runner retreat back to his base or suffer a double play. Once the runner touches a base, you can't move him.

Press B and the appropriate key on the direction pad to make your players dive for balls. Hit B alone and they leap up to snag line drives.

Fast Pitch Mode

     Game #3:

> DmgvyMM5XlYDmJ
> mNPXb7ØxØdLgXZG

     Game #4:

> LgtwwRG7XtRHlR
> 3R14rvwk2jbkljh

     Game#5: Championship game

> LgtwwRG7MtdHTR
> 7R941vØv24y342J

Slow Pitch Mode

     Game #3:

> jljtNLRYWjrbJW
> nDl87n2rrmP5jbh

     Game #4:

> dpp8TTJTRhrWNV
> tJxzvØ84zØkzXql

     Game #5: Championship game

> vlkyVQKTlplbQQ
> vB751w6w8x39yxT

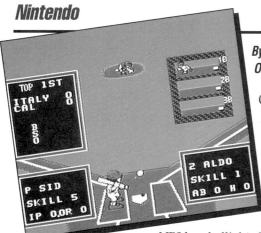

By SNK
One or Two Players (simultaneous)

Oh, I can hear you Big League hardball freaks snickering already. Hey, eat some peanuts and Cracker Jack! Little League's no joke! And Little League Baseball from SNK definitely has the muscle to stand out among NES baseball's big boys.

You get your choice of 16 teams to play, eight domestic teams and eight foreign teams from Asia and Europe. In One-Player mode you play the computer in an international tournament. For Two Players, you each have a squad in the tourney. All games are seven innings long.

To help you pick a team, a Power Analysis screen enables you to see how teams rate on hitting, pitching, overall defense, and running.

When you're up to bat move around in the box, control your swing, even hit a bunt. Pitchers can burn 'em in, slow 'em down, spin 'em right, or curve 'em left. Just don't throw the ball in too tight or you'll bean the batter (and boy, do they look hurt!). On defense, all players can dive for balls or jump up to snare line drives. Infielders can tag one base and throw to another. A great defensive plus here is the ability to move players into pre-set defensive shifts, for example, to defend against pull hitters or bunts.

Don't let the Little League label fool you. The video baseball here is top notch, as good as any around. Little League Baseball is guaranteed to send some Big League baseball carts back to the minors. Bye, bye Baby!

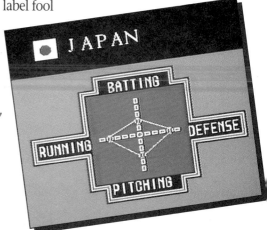

Hot ProTips

⭐ Korea, California, Texas, and New York are strong and well-balanced teams.

⭐ Bunting can be an effective offensive weapon. There's a kind of drag bunt that catches the defense off-guard, although the contact accuracy is low. And there's a sure-fire bunt where the batter's usually thrown out but runners always advance.

⭐ If you're at bat with no outs, bunt. Keep bunting until you make an out. The computer has a hard time defending against this strategy. The top of the order is usually the most effective.

⭐ Versus the computer, try a squeeze play with the bases loaded. If it works, do it again!

⭐ You can put real movement on your pitches by pressing Left and then Right just after you throw the ball. Try pressing them as fast as you can to really fool a batter.

⭐ To throw to a base, select the base by pressing the directional pad and then pressing A. But to throw in a hurry, press both buttons simultaneously.

⭐ A great defensive plus in this game is the ability to move players into pre-set defensive shifts – for example, to defend against pull hitters or bunts.

⭐ Columbus may have discovered America, but he didn't discover America's favorite pastime. Italy is the weakest team in the cart, a definite cellar-dweller.

By Tengen
One or Two Players (simultaneous)

Here's the baseball action that started it all – the one, the only, the original RBI. With permission from the Major League Players Association, this game uses the names and likenesses of real baseball players. This means the ten different teams in the Tengen league can have lineups that include the likes of Reggie Jackson, Fernando Valenzuela, and Willie McGee. Stats and abilities have been structured to give each player the strengths and weaknesses he had in the 1986 and 1987 seasons. You'll have to use your knowledge of real players and teams to manage your lineup effectively.

The teams you can choose from include Detroit, California, Houston, San Francisco, and even the American and the National League All-Star teams. In One-Player mode you compete with the computer for the pennant in a nine game season. If you want to go head-to-head with a friend, you can each pick your favorite team and then compete in your own best-of-seven series.

At bat you can hit anything from a home run to a bunt to a line drive. If you manage to get on base you control your base runners. After three outs you'll find yourself on the mound, on second base, in center field, and in the dugout – all at once!

Between its popularity in Japan and its popularity as a coin op in the U.S., RBI is one of the best known of the pack of baseball titles available for video gamers. It's guaranteed baseball entertainment.

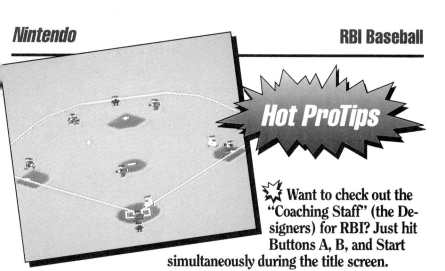

Want to check out the "Coaching Staff" (the Designers) for RBI? Just hit Buttons A, B, and Start simultaneously during the title screen.

The American and National League Teams are two of the hottest in RBI. The National League Team has very fast runners. Boston and New York are also tough squads.

Check out the player ratings to get a feel for the strength of your team. Each player is rated on an A-E scale (A being the strongest) in two areas: Speed and Contact. The speed rating indicates how good the player is at stealing a base. Contact has to do with the ability to get base hits as opposed to fouls and fly balls. The ratings are fairly consistent with the real abilities of players in the 1987/88 season.

To improve your reaction time when you're up to bat in RBI, try the following: Move as far forward (towards the pitcher) on the plate as you can. Tap Button A lightly once to get your bat into the first position. Now you're ready to swing and knock it out of the ball park.

Remember, to make the game more realistic each batter has a different batting average. Don't forget to check out the stats. When you're on the mound you'll be facing anything from pitchers who can only hit .150 to sluggers who hit above .300. Pick your pitches accordingly.

Each of the teams has a bullpen consisting of two starting pitchers and two relievers. Starting pitchers can keep speed and power on their pitches for more innings than the relievers.

Pace your starting pitcher well and he'll go four or five innings. Throw too many fastballs or screwballs and you'll find he burns out quickly. Remember, you've only got two relievers and if your starter gets tired too quickly you may have trouble making it to the end of the game with your relievers. Pace your starter by mixing some slower stuff in with your faster pitches.

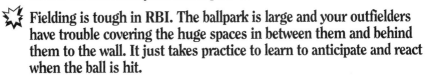 Fielding is tough in RBI. The ballpark is large and your outfielders have trouble covering the huge spaces in between them and behind them to the wall. It just takes practice to learn to anticipate and react when the ball is hit.

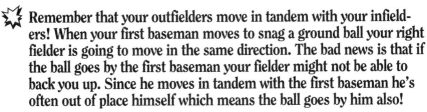 Remember that your outfielders move in tandem with your infielders! When your first baseman moves to snag a ground ball your right fielder is going to move in the same direction. The bad news is that if the ball goes by the first baseman your fielder might not be able to back you up. Since he moves in tandem with the first baseman he's often out of place himself which means the ball goes by him also!

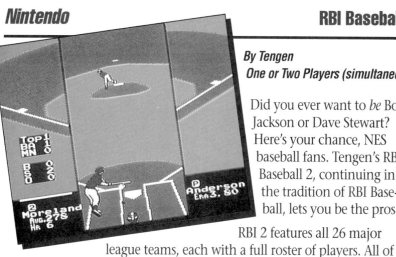

By Tengen
One or Two Players (simultaneous)

Did you ever want to *be* Bo Jackson or Dave Stewart? Here's your chance, NES baseball fans. Tengen's RBI Baseball 2, continuing in the tradition of RBI Baseball, lets you be the pros.

RBI 2 features all 26 major league teams, each with a full roster of players. All of your favorites are here: Jose Canseco, Dwight Gooden, Will Clark, even Omar Vizquel! You can choose any National or American League team. You can even play one of the 1989 All-Star squads.

RBI 2 has One Player and Two Player options as well as a Password mode to enable you to play a full season (one game against every team in the division). In addition, a Watch mode provides you with the best seat in the house for a computer-controlled matchup.

RBI 2 is similar to the original RBI baseball in terms of gameplay. This time around the game uses the teams and statistics from the 1989 season. Just as in the original, you get to see what it's like to step up to the plate as Ricky Henderson, pitch the ball like Nolan Ryan, and catch a pop fly just like Ozzie Smith. But when you're in your favorites' video game shoes, it's up to you to make all of the right moves.

RBI 2's great selling points are the American and the National Leagues. How many of us wouldn't give our right arm for the chance to play on and manage a major league team? Well, no need to sacrifice your pitching arm. RBI 2 lets you play and manage your home town favorites. Is your home team headed for the cellar already? Batter up!

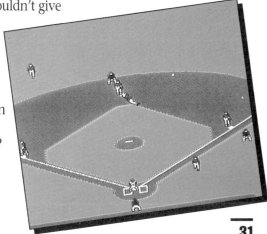

 As with the original, you ought to study the stats of all of the 1989 teams before you pick your squad. Of course, if you're a real fan, throw strategy out the window and just go with your favorites.

Since RBI 2 uses the teams and statistics from the 1989 season the division winners Oakland, Toronto, Chicago, and San Francisco are the strongest clubs.

The most consistently effective pitch against computer batters is the inside out fast slider.

The most effective way to keep your team out of trouble is to have your pitcher throw nothing but curveballs, with the occasional heater mixed in. There are several great forkball pitchers here, but this pitch can be dangerous if it doesn't drop.

Most pitchers can hurl a strong breaking ball for two or three innings, so switch pitchers about that often. This pitching strategy is particularly effective with teams such as the Oakland A's who have monster pitching staffs.

Forget the bunt; it's very difficult. The defense reacts very quickly and batters can't place bunts.

Finish a full season undefeated and you'll get a special password that lets you play against the most powerful team in RBI 2 – The Tengen Team. This team is loaded with powerhitters, basestealers, and incredible pitchers. It takes your very best, plus some luck, to beat these guys!

Here are some passwords that let you practice against the Tengen team:

Toronto Vs. Tengen:	F0OMB6AP
Detroit Vs. Tengen:	R0OMB6AP
Minnesota Vs. Tengen:	SI0MB6AP
Cleveland Vs. Tengen:	V0OMB6AP
Boston Vs. Tengen:	J0OMB6AP
Seattle Vs. Tengen:	SA0MB6AP
California Vs. Tengen:	SU0MB6AP
Oakland Vs. Tengen:	SE0MB6AP

By Sega of America
One or Two Players (simultaneous)

Hey, the Dodgers can't win a pennant every year, but you can win big with Dodger manager Tommy Lasorda's top-flight video game. This was the first 16-bit baseball cart on the market, and it set a high standard for 16-bit sports fans right off the bat.

Play alone or with a friend. Choose from any of the 26 major league teams. The game uses all of the real-life city names, but the stats and the player names are specific to this game.

Once you take the field, game play follows standard baseball rules. The password feature enables you to take your team all the way through a season to the World Series. The game also tracks all of the other teams in the league simultaneously.

Batters in the game are rated according to batting average, homeruns, running speed, and fielding and throwing ability. Pitchers are rated by ERA (Earned Run Average), curve-throwing ability, stamina, top throwing speed, and the distance a hit pitch will travel. All the ratings make this game a challenge to your managerial ability as well as your gaming skill because you're calling the shots from the dugout.

The option screen enables you to decide how tough your computer opponent will be. You can play a pitcher's duel, a batter's slugfest, or a normal game. Decide whether there'll be fielding errors and determine how the wind will affect hit balls. This game covers just about every detail, right down to umps who shout "safe" or "out." So grab a bat, whip out the pine tar, step up to the plate, and play ball!

Hot ProTips

⭐ Pay close attention to team stats and ratings before you play a full season. Learn which teams are the strongest. For example, the Oakland A's are stacked with sluggers. The San Francisco Giants are well-balanced with good hitting and steady pitching. Of course, you can play your favorites, but check out all the teams if you want to win the Pennant.

⭐ This game has very long and complicated passwords. Take special care to note passwords down carefully or you might find yourself starting your season all over again.

⭐ Use sound pitching strategy. Mix up speed and location, especially when you play the computer. Keep using the same pitch in the same location and you'll get tagged.

⭐ Hitting is the toughest part of the game and beginners should make it easy on themselves. At the start of the game, select the Options menu from the Game Select screen. Set CPU to Easy, make Type a Batter's Game, and switch the Wind off. When you learn how to hit, set the game back to normal mode.

⭐ It's difficult to hit against a good pitcher in normal mode. But lefties can almost always bunt down the 3rd base line safely, if they're leading off or there's a man on base. Hit A to square up for the bunt (wait until the pitch is thrown or the defense knows you're bunting), then press the directional controller to the left and bunt down the line.

Play any team you want in the World Series:

H_ _flmnjiaVXhLQZPqBCVA
AB

Select your team by putting one of the following in Blank A:

D	(Detroit)	Q	(Texas)
E	(Toronto)	R	(St. Louis)
F	(Milwaukee)	S	(New York Mets)
G	(New York Yankees)	T	(Montreal)
H	(Boston)	U	(Philadelphia)
I	(Baltimore)	V	(Pittsburg)
J	(Cleveland)	W	(Chicago Cubs)
K	(Minnesota)	X	(San Francisco)
L	(Kansas City)	Y	(Cincinnati)
M	(Oakland)	Z	(Houston)
N	(Seattle)	a	(Los Angeles)
O	(Chicago White Sox)	b	(Atlanta)
P	(California)	c	(San Diego)

* Milwaukee, Minnesota, Philadelphia, and Houston must be played versus one of the following teams: Milwaukee, Philadelphia, Baltimore, San Francisco, Kansas City, Los Angeles, Chicago White Sox, or St. Louis.

Use Blank B to select your opponent by putting one letter higher in the alphabet than the team's regular letter. For example, Detroit is "D," so if you wished to have Detroit as your opponent you would put "E" in blank B. Oakland is "M." To play Oakland enter "N" in blank B.

To play in a strange fantasy league enter the following code and choose
your team:

VU9lrstpomXcZ
TiebrHWyW

By Hudson Soft/NEC
One or Two Players (simultaneous)

With one eye on the pitcher you inch away from the base. As he hurls the pitch you take off for second. The catcher throws the ball and you slide towards the plate. When the dust clears the ump yells, "You're out!" Oh well, next time!

It's World Class Baseball action! You'll feel you're in the infield or the dugout calling the shots right from the beginning. Pick from 12 different teams, each with a total of 25 active players. If you see some weaknesses in your lineup, use the Edit mode to swap players within your team and get your lineup just the way you want it.

Play the computer or a friend in a one-game series or try to beat five of the 12 league teams and take home the pennant. If you're feeling lazy, you can always sit back and watch two computer goliaths go at it while you enjoy your peanuts and popcorn.

Throw sizzling pitches at your opponent – including curve balls, fast balls, and sliders. You'll also get a chance to show off your fancy moves in the outfield. When you're at bat it's up to you whether you strike out or hit a triple. And don't forget to manage your team – replace tired players, bring in pinch hitters, or call time-outs!

When you hit a home run you'll hear the roar of the ecstatic crowd. On a less pleasant note, you'll also hear the umps calling you out! For pennant fever all year round, World Class Baseball is the name of the game.

Hot ProTips

🌟 Check out the Watch mode! It's a good way to look for strategies and learn to better predict certain pitches.

🌟 During the Select Team Mode you can pick which team goes up to bat or into the outfield first. Just press any direction on the pad to move the bat to the desired team to indicate who's up first. This works on all play modes except the Pennant Mode.

🌟 The World Champs are tough to beat! They're loaded with power-hitters and pitchers who throw at 120 mph! You'll need to play a near perfect game to beat these guys. Here are a few ProTips to help you beat the champs! Try using these with the password that puts you up against the champs as the Tokyo Ninjas:

1) Replace your current shortstop, Takas, with the farm fielder, Oishi. Takas has hands of stone and will make several costly errors. Oishi is steady and a switch hitter with good speed. Replace one of your light-hitting pinch hitters with Takas.

2) Replace your pitcher, Junko (in the bullpen), with Ando, from the farm team. Ando has a good right curve, a pitch the computer's right-handed batters have trouble with.

3) Use Kondo as your pitcher. Throw right-handed batters right curveballs, moving them at the batter, and then sharply to the right when they're halfway to the plate. The computer batters will usually not swing at the first pitch and ground the second pitch to one of your infielders.

4) Pitching to left-handed batters with Kondo is more challenging. Try throwing fastballs inside to the left-handed hitters. Be careful. Fastballs too far over the plate will be hit hard!

Try playing with the Super Team!! This trick is only for the Two Player Mode. Let your friend select his team first. Choose your team and as you leave the team selection, screen push Button I and Select. Now you control the best team in the league!

Become the World Champs with the Tokyo Ninjas!

D7E8	Two Wins
5771	Three Wins
E450	Four Wins
20D8	Pennant Win
0E03	Vs. The World Champs

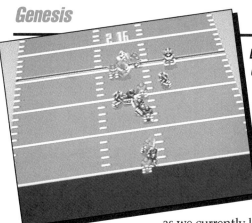

By Sega of America
One or Two Players (simultaneous)

Football is a game filled with pressure situations. But when you're playing with a ball that can explode at any minute, pressure takes on an entirely different meaning! Yes, Cyberball is not football as we currently know it. The game eliminates drawbacks such as escalating player salaries and constant injuries by simply replacing humans with robots.

In Cyberball you choose from 28 teams in two different leagues. You'll play a full 16-game season, just like the NFL. If your team is good enough, it's on to the playoffs and perhaps even the championship.

Cyberball follows the basics of football. A team of players tries to move the ball up the field via passing or running plays. Of course there are a few differences...The ball is not almond-shaped, and isn't made of pigskin. It's metallic like the players, and it gets hotter the longer a team takes to get to a certain point on the field. Other differences include six three-minute periods (rather than the traditional 15-minute quarters), earning money for crossing midfield on offense and scoring points, seven players per side, and, of course, the all-robot half-time show!

You don't have to worry about player strikes or injuries, but you do have to worry about team members who take too much punishment, overheat and explode – not something you want to have happen as you drive towards the goal line! In Cyberball you have to be a good coach – but it helps if you're a skillful mechanic as well. We've seen the future and it's Cyberball!

If you're playing in League Mode try to save your money for the championship game. When you buy a player upgrade you can only use it in an upcoming game. The upgrades do not carry over to future contests during the season.

You can accumulate a maximum of $999,999. Once you reach this point you no longer accumulate funds. Take advantage of this by spending down every couple of games, leaving yourself enough games to get back to the $999,999 level before the championship.

To avoid the computer opponent's blitz (which usually occurs on first down when the ball is cool), try the "Wide Angle" running play. This is an outside pitch to either the right or the left side running back – both of whom are out of reach of the blitzers.

One of the most effective plays against the computer opponent is the "Alley Oop" pass play. This is a toss to the running back coming out of the back field. The defenders usually concentrate on the wide receivers and ignore the running back.

Your defense is a killer if you buy the "power boost" for your safety. Choose a long defensive formation and select "Nickel." Now control the left safety. When the ball is hiked hit your turbo button and blast through the opponent's line. You'll get a lot of quarterback sacks and the rest of your defense will be able to stop any play the computer runs – just in case you don't tackle the quarterback.

When running the ball try to think like a running back. Good running backs don't charge into the tacklers, they try to fake them out. You have to do the same thing in Cyberball – dodge, weave, and fake. You'll be surprised at how much daylight you create by pausing or faking.

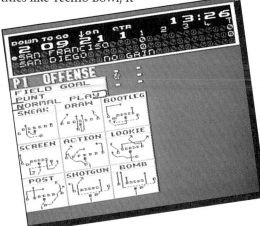

By Tradewest
One or Two Players (simultaneous)

So you say football's your game, huh? Well, it's John Elway's, too, and Denver's star quarterback and two-time AFC Player of the Year has put his moniker on this football cart from Tradewest. An arcade hit, this game lets you strap on Elway's helmet and step behind the line of scrimmage to see how the big boys play football – without the grass stains, broken bones, and other assorted injuries that John faces every week.

Before the kickoff one or two players choose from 14 different teams, representing famous NFL football cities. There's no password or save function in this cart. Just pick your team and go head-to-head against the computer or another player in a one-time match up.

This game focuses on the quarterback although you play defense, too. You call all the plays in the huddle. You also learn to read the defense so that if you don't like the way things look, you can change the play at the line. There are nine different offensive plays to choose from – six passing plays and three running plays. Run them from either side of the field for a total of 18 different options. On defense you'll have to learn to read offense and then call one of six different defensive plays.

Although John Elway's Quarterback doesn't feature the in-depth strategy of more complex gridiron titles like Tecmo Bowl, it does feature, among other things, fast action, arcade-style play, and, of course, John Elway! Let your thumb become the strongest arm in football!

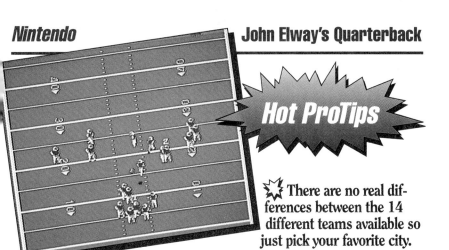

Hot ProTips

☆ There are no real differences between the 14 different teams available so just pick your favorite city.

☆ When you kick off, press Up on the control pad and simultaneously press Button B rapidly. Your men will form a V formation, cruise up the field, and tackle your opponent around his own ten yard line!

☆ Your best offensive strategy is to avoid getting sacked and throw the ball long. Your receiver will catch the ball the majority of the time, if you can loft it to him before a defender takes you down.

☆ When you drop back to pass, move the pass arrow way up the field towards the middle. Now throw the ball. Your receivers will almost always catch up to the ball no matter how far ahead of them it is!

☆ To create super-fast receivers on offense, try the following trick: When you're in the play select mode, move the cursor to the Normal/Reverse window and leave it there until time expires for picking a play. Now your receivers are supercharged! Throw the ball up-field and let them catch up to it for a sure touchdown.

☆ On defense remember that you can press Button A to make a diving tackle or go for an interception if you're close enough to the ball. Pressing Button B enables you to switch to the next defender closest to the ball handler.

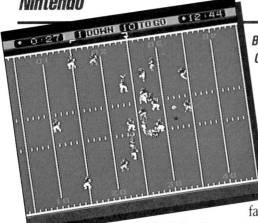

By LJN
One or Two Players (simultaneous)

If you want to play in the big leagues, with the real teams and players of the NFL, then NFL Football just might be for you. This NES cart is officially licensed by the NFL and features all of your favorite American and National Football Conference teams – from the Miami Dolphins to the Los Angeles Rams.

One Player can take on the computer, and Two Players can take on each other in one of four game options: AFC, NFC, Interconference, or Super Bowl. Choose your own team package and then upgrade and customize your team to give them the winning edge.

Once the coin is tossed and the whistle sounds it's kickoff time! You call the shots from the sidelines as coach, picking your plays from actual NFL Playbook offensive and defensive plays. You're also right in the middle of the onfield action, because you're everybody from the quarterback to the linebacker to the punter. This means that when your team has the ball you call your play and formation in from the sideline, and then you call audibles, control the snap, run, pass, kick, and generally do it all! When you're on defense you select your defensive formation, and even adjust it at the last moment when you see the offensive lineup.

Complete with a number of complicated gameplay options, NFL Football offers video gamers authentic football action with their favorite teams. Although it may not be the number one title for the electronic gridiron, there's enough play action to satisfy any die-hard fan.

Hot ProTips

On defense, just as in real football, you can bump the receivers within 10 yards of the line of scrimmage. Smash into the receivers with your defensive player to knock them off their pass routes.

The "Saw: Run" and "Saw: Pass" defenses bunch all of your defenders on the line of scrimmage. Only use these plays in goal line and short yardage situations. These plays often leave your opponent's wide receivers open for long passes.

Running plays such as "Slash Left" and "Slash Right" are usually good for at least a seven-yard gain versus the computer, assuming your running back has an "A" rating.

It is important to move your receivers back to the ball on a pass play. This helps prevent interceptions and gets your team more completions.

Make sure you choose a team package that has an "A" or "B" rating for your key offensive players – your quarterback, running back, and wide receivers. Package #1 meets these requirements.

Try a "flea-flicker" play. Choose "Play-Action Pass Left" or "Play-Action Pass Right," pitch the ball to your running back; then throw the ball to an open receiver. Chances are you'll catch the defense off guard.

By Tecmo
One or Two Players (simultaneous)

Grab your shoulder pads. You're going to need all of the protection you can get once you step onto the Tecmo Bowl field for bone-crunching gridiron action as player, coach, and spectator all rolled into one.

In Tecmo Bowl you can square off against the computer, playing against the rest of the league as you work towards a winning season, or go head-to-head against a friend with the team of your choice. If you don't feel like getting grass stains on your jersey, choose the Coach Mode. As head coach you'll call the plays from the side lines for your computer team.

Each of the 12 Tecmo Bowl teams represents a real NFC city and uses the actual player roster. Since the game is licensed by the National Football League, a team that has a strong passing game or a great defense has similar skills in Tecmo Bowl.

Once you take the field with your team you'll be doing anything and everything but sitting on the bench. From the opening kickoff to the final gun you're the coach...and also the quarterback, linebacker, center, and the rest of the squad.

READER'S TOP 20 CHOICE

Tecmo Bowl also has crowd noises, voice effects, and graphics so real your muscles will ache. But that's just the icing on the cake. It takes more than a Sunday afternoon quarterback to win at Tecmo Bowl – it's the real football strategist who'll succeed. When it's draft time and you're looking for a football cart to add to your Nintendo line-up, Tecmo Football is an excellent first round choice for any football fan.

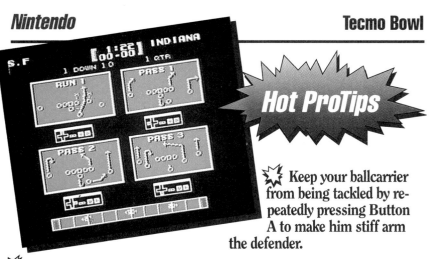

★ Keep your ballcarrier from being tackled by repeatedly pressing Button A to make him stiff arm the defender.

★ Press Button B when you're on defense to attempt diving tackles.

★ Here are some team selection tips:

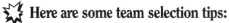

New York Giants – One of the most powerful teams in Tecmo Bowl, the Giants have the top defensive player in the league, Lawrence Taylor. Not only is Taylor a ferocious tackler, he's extremely agile. Even if he misses a tackle, he can get right up and catch the runner from behind. An especially effective defense using the Giants is to select "Pass #2" defense, choose Taylor as the player you control, and blitz the quarterback. You'll usually be able to sack the QB, nail the runner in the backfield, or hold the offensive team to a short gain. The Giants click on offense when they mix runs with short passes over the middle to Mark Bavarro, their Tight End (Pass Play #1).

San Francisco 49ers – Called the Team of the Eighties by many, the Niners feature an almost unstoppable offense that features the strong throwing arm of quarterback Joe Montana. Some Niner offensive plays even feature four receivers. Roger Craig heads up a strong running game. On defense the safety, Ronnie Lott, is one of the better players to control. He's quick and a ferocious hitter.

Chicago Bears – The 1988 edition of the Chicago Bears is highlighted by their tenacious defense. Led by Mike Singletary and Richard Dent, the Bears D is usually a nightmare for the opposing offense. This Bears team also features the ultra-slick moves of Walter Payton, one of the greatest running backs of all time. Payton can either outmaneuver or simply run over any defensive back that gets in his way. A good defensive strategy with the Bears is to select a run defense and control the safety, Dave Duerson, to guard against the pass.

Play Tecmo Bowl as Chicago against an Invisible Team!

397BFFA5

Try these passwords to pit a team against itself!

Chicago Vs. Chicago	697BFFA5
Washington Vs. Washington	997FBFA5
Denver Vs. Denver	CFBFF7AØ

Try some Championship Games:

Los Angeles Vs. Washington	967FBFA5
Seattle Vs. Washington	937FBFA5
San Francisco Vs. Washington	9C7FBFA5
San Francisco Vs. Denver	1DAFF7A6
Chicago Vs. Los Angeles	A89FDFA8

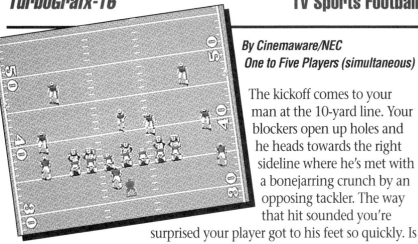

By Cinemaware/NEC
One to Five Players (simultaneous)

The kickoff comes to your man at the 10-yard line. Your blockers open up holes and he heads towards the right sideline where he's met with a bonejarring crunch by an opposing tackler. The way that hit sounded you're surprised your player got to his feet so quickly. Is this a day at an NFL stadium? Nope, just something similar – Cinemaware's T.V. Sports Football for the TurboGrafx-16.

In T.V. Sports Football you play the role of coach, quarterback, linebacker, and just about everything else. You can decide whether to play an exhibition game or a full season using one of the eight teams. With the Turbo-Tap up to five people can play at once – up to four on any one team.

On offense you call the play (pass or run) and then decide how much control over the quarterback you'll have. If you do nothing at all, when the ball is snapped the computer will take over the helm and run the play for you.

Realistic passing controls make T.V. Sports Football more difficult than other gridiron games. To complete a pass to your receivers, you must time and aim your throw – just like a real quarterback. Initially, less experienced players will find this frustrating, but with practice it becomes one of the features that makes this game so much fun.

T.V. Sports Football is the first football game for the TurboGrafx-16 and it sets high standards for future pigskin releases. Don't forget to wave "hi" to Mom when the T.V. camera's on you.

Hot ProTips

⚡ If you press Button I rapidly, your ball carrier is more likely to dodge tackles and outrun defenders.

⚡ Defense versus the computer: Choose a 3-4 setup and select "Pass Defense." The key to shutting down the computer on offense is to SHADOW the computer's quarterback with your middle linebacker. In this defensive setup the rest of your players will adequately cover the computer's receivers so he can't throw a pass. Your job is to make sure the computer's quarterback doesn't get by you with the ball.

⚡ The trick to passing on offense is to throw the ball slightly ahead of where the receiver is running. "Lead" a receiver just like a real NFL quarterback.

⚡ On defense, if a hole opens up in the middle of the line, blitz the quarterback. You'll force him to run for his life!

⚡ NEVER call a "Goaline Defense." It leaves too many receivers wide open.

⚡ Here's an easy trick that you can do up to three times per half that's almost guaranteed to rack up a lot of yardage for your team. First, on offense in a third and long situation call for a "Kick." Next, press Button II to call time out. Quickly press Button II again to bring up the play selection screen, call for a "Shotgun Formation", and choose a pass play. This trick usually leaves the computer stuck in a punt return or punt block formation, leaving your receivers wide open for an easy completion!

The Hounds

BFSGM	(1-0)
LCBSW	(2-0)
NKRPV	(3-0)
GEFGWY	(4-0)
BKTBSVTF	(5-0)
ENLTVKWRQ	(6-0)

The Thunderbolts

GCE	(1-0)
BLUAT	(2-0)
FSIMBG	(3-0)

By Vic Tokai
One or Two Players (simultaneous)

Video round ball seems to come in a variety of court sizes and player numbers. All Pro Basketball combines five-on-five full-court action with a half-court screen view.

All-Pro style B-ball features several different play options. Go head-to-head with a friend in a one-game contest. Feeling lazy? Watch two computer teams battle it out on court. If you choose league competition your task is to lead your team to the league championship. In One Player league play you battle the computer in a 35-game season. In Two Player league play you and a buddy team up to battle the computer teams. Choose your squad from eight professional rosters – ranging from the New York Slicks to the San Francisco Bayriders. Each team has their own strengths and weaknesses. Pick the team that plays your style of game, or just go with your favorite city!

When the scene is set, the game begins with a jump ball and then it's non-stop no-holds-barred B-ball. On offense you're the team – running, jumping, jump passing, shooting, and even going for spectacular three-pointers or slam dunks. On defense make a steal or grab a rebound. And remember this is real video game basketball. You get called for fouls and your teammates get tired. When their health and stamina gets low it's up to you to put them on the bench for a rest.

Altogether All-Pro Basketball is five-on-five hoops that includes most of the finer points of video game B-ball – including a halftime show with some very perky cheerleaders. Rah, rah, sis, boom, bah!

Hot ProTips

⭐ To win the Championship Tournament you must beat all seven teams five times each.

⭐ The Los Angeles Breakers and the Seattle Sonics are well-balanced strong teams. San Francisco is the weakest team. The computer usually picks New York as its team.

⭐ Nobody can stop a jump pass. Just press B then A.

⭐ Baseline jumpers are your most effective shots with any team.

⭐ The manual says you have a 24-second shot clock, but the cart's timer runs slower than real time. It actually takes a minute and a half in real time before you get called for a shot clock violation. If you can keep passing the ball around that long, you usually draw a foul.

⭐ When the close-up screen appears as you block a dunk attempt, press the control pad in the direction of the block and hold it there until the normal view appears. This enables your man to continue through the block and grab the rebound.

⭐ To improve three-point shot accuracy, don't shoot when you're right up on the line. Take a step away from the three-point line and then shoot.

⭐ Height isn't an advantage. Short players block shots as well as tall players and tall players have weak jump shots.

⭐ On defense versus the computer, if two of your players move up on the player inbounding the ball, press A rapidly (to flip-flop player control) and you can force a 10-second violation (and a turnover).

⭐ Don't bother to make substitutions until half-time. That's usually when your players start to tire.

⭐ If the computer's man gets up close to your ballhandler, he usually steals the ball. Learn to pass before that happens.

In a two-player game one person can control four players at a time. When you and your friend play the computer, one person should race down the court whenever the ball changes hands while the other manages the rest of the team. On offense, the free man can get open close to the basket for a high-percentage shot. On defense, he prevents the other team from fastbreaking on you.

Here's a password that enables you to begin the Championship Tournament as Seattle Sonics, undefeated and half way through:

> NFJNKMMJMJFQ

Here's a password that puts you in the championship game as the LA Breakers with a 34 win, 0 loss record:

> BEOLEHPPHRMR

By Konami
One or Two Players (simultaneous)

Video hoopsters eveywhere rank Double Dribble as one of the top all time sports carts. The game features fast paced, action packed, sneaker squeaking B-ball that's hard to beat.

Double Dribble's on court action pits teams of five players against one another in a full court game. Play against the computer or against a friend. Set the computer to easy, medium, or difficult. Choose from four different teams, each with its own special abilities.

Game play is divided into four periods – you choose from 5-, 10-, 20-, or 30-minute periods. Game time is half of real time – a 10-minute period is actually five minutes long. On court you control your team and make sure they have all of the right moves – you'll need to run, jump, shoot, pass, make free throws, guard, steal the ball, and make some wicked standard, reverse, and even one-handed dunk shots.

READER'S TOP 20 CHOICE

The refs call a tight game and you'll have to follow the rules. Penalties include traveling, blocking, and pushing. You'll also lose the ball if you fail to inbound it within the time limit, hold it for more than five seconds without dribbling, or pass it into the backcourt.

Winning is easy – simply score more buckets than the opposing team! Scoring is standard – two points from inside the three point line and three points from outside of it. It takes heart and it takes team work, but if things don't work out, you can always watch the half-time show – complete with pom-pom-waving cheerleaders and your very own mascot!

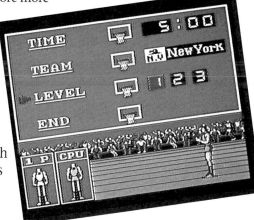

Hot ProTips

⭐ When you've got possession of the ball, move it down court with accurate passing. You'll almost always be in position to score, and often, to dunk the ball. Hang on to the ball too long and you'll have it stolen in the blink of an eye. Keep it fast and keep it moving!

⭐ The kind of dunk you slam home is controlled by your position and jump. You'll go up for a standard two-handed dunk when you shoot near the basket, and a one-hander if you shoot near and jump higher. For a spectacular reverse dunk, go for it from right underneath the basket!

⭐ Shoot from the court's X-markers for the greatest accuracy in your jump shots.

⭐ The Boston Frogs are really hot offensively with mean inside shots and accuracy you won't believe. The New York Eagles shoot well from the outside, scoring quite a few 3-pointers, but they're not as good from the inside.

⭐ On defense just keep hitting A and B simultaneously! Button B puts you in control of the defensive player nearest the ball and Button A steals the ball. This method produces a lot of steals – and also a lot of wild shots from the backcourt because you're often not aware that you've stolen the ball until you find yourself shooting it from a ridiculous distance!

⭐ The Chicago Ox are the hottest team when it comes to stealing the ball.

⭐ When your opponent inbounds the ball near your basket, go for the steal by watching which player on your opponent's team is flashing. It's a relatively easy way to grab the ball and go for a quick basket before the other team knows what hit them. However, this move works both ways. When you're inbounding the ball, keep your opponent on his toes by switching your throwing direction back and forth so you don't reveal where you're going to pass the ball.

By Jaleco
One or Two Players (simultaneous)

There's basketball and then there's Hoops! Hoops is basketball like it's played on the streets, complete with a crew of off-beat players who get together for a half-court pick-up game at the city playground.

Lace up your high-top sneaks and head out to your neighborhood court to pick from several different play options. Go one-on-one or two-on-two against the computer or a friend in Shoot for Possession or Around the World. Pick either a Western or an Eastern court. You decide what the winning score will be and who gets side-out after a basket.

Pick your alter ego or a partner in the case of two-on-two from eight of the craziest hoopsters ever to hit the court. There's Barbie the blonde bombshell. She's an all-American girl who likes to run with the big boys. Wiz is one four-eyes who's smart and fast. He plays a thinking man's game. And of course there's Bomber who likes to drop in a bucket from way outside.

On court this is down-and-dirty no-holds-barred basketball. First off you shoot for possession of the ball. Once the action begins your basic goal is to get the basketball through the hoop – any way you can. Most players are aggressive, especially when the computer plays. Pushing and charging are the most commonly called fouls and you're going to get the ball stolen more times than you can believe. Hey, it will all be worth it when you break away for the basket and drive home a slam dunk – that is, if a defender isn't there to knock it away.

Like we said, this is b-ball like it's played on the streets. You gotta be lean, mean, and a basketball machine!

Hot ProTips

⭐ Several of the Hoops players are hot long-distance shooters and can hit an impossible shot from half-court. When your player has the ball at the baseline, move him to the left rear corner. Shoot a jump shot, releasing the ball when the player is at the peak of his jump. If done correctly, it will swish right through the net every time! Try this trick with Bomber. All other players have a spot from where they're extremely accurate. Find yours, and on defense, keep your man away from his!

⭐ For one-on-one play, we like Face. He has height, he can steal, and he has a good shooting touch. Mr. Doc is a good second choice, but Face's defense is stronger. Face and Mr. Doc make a well-rounded two-on-two team.

⭐ In a one-on-one versus the computer, play smart "D." Keep your player near to or inside of the key. Don't overplay your man, he'll usually burn you for two.

⭐ In a one-on-one game, by keeping your defender under the basket you can block or alter an attempted slam-dunk automatically. This defense, known as Cherry Picking, works especially well if the player under the basket is Face, Mr. Doc, or Zap.

⭐ When you grab a defensive rebound or you steal the ball inside of the key, you have to take it out to the baseline before you can shoot. The baseline is approximately the top of the key. Watch the arrow under your player – it disappears when you reach the baseline.

⭐ Here's a good move for one-on-one versus the computer: When you take the ball out of bounds, wait the defender out. After a while, he usually turns his back and retreats to the basket. That's when you can make your move!

Here's a play for two-on-two versus the computer. Whenever you inbound the ball, move the player with the ball a few quick steps in any direction. Then immediately make a jump pass by pressing B and then A. Your other man is usually in good position near the hoop. Try to can a quick jumper.

 In two-on-two, try double teaming the ballhandler once in a while. Sometimes you can get an easy steal.

 As in most basketball carts, fouling is a good defensive tactic.

Passwords

Passwords for the team of Zap and Barbie:

1. AELJFBNAO	8. OXABPWQRT
2. FHQJRHUMU	9. FMTFGONPL
3. MVYZNPOPT	10. PQYDZZPDA
4. BIPBCFJQO	11. FJHOKQSIM
5. GHPUQLGRI	12. LNWPXXAPA
6. DHFMIJQGG	13. NWZAOAPAA
7. EGPIQLTLM	14. MTAMNAUMM

By Milton Bradley
One or Two Players (simultaneous)

The 24-second clock is down to 6 and Jordan has Bird pinned in the corner. Bird jumps. Jordan jumps. Steal! Jordan pivots, races for the basket, skywalks the last 15 feet, and jams home a 360 dunk. It's one-on-one with two top super-stars, Michael Jordan and Larry Bird.

In One on One you go head to head against the computer or a friend in a variety of different modes. If you choose classic one-on-one basketball, you'll play a game with four 2-, 5-, 8- or 12-minute periods. In One on One 15 or 11, play a game straight through until one player scores either 15 or 11 points. Between games of One on One you can try your hand at Jordan's Slam Dunk Contest or Bird's Three-Point Shooting Contest.

Your first decision is whether to be Jordan or Bird. Next, if you're playing the computer, choose one of four difficulty levels, ranging from schoolyard to professional! Finally, set the game parameters such as winner's outs or fouls.

Now the fun begins. Learn to back your player into position, then blow by for the dunk or shoot a fade-away jumper to light up the scoreboard. Play smart defense to keep your opponent from scoring and be sure to block out so you get all the rebounds. Check your stats at the end of each quarter to see how you're doing.

This cart has something for every hoopster – whether you feel like going one-on-one with a friend, shooting the sweet shot with Bird, or taking to the sky with Air Jordan.

Hot ProTips

💥 Both Bird and Jordan have a quick first step in the One on One competition, so faking when you inbound the ball is a slick move. For example, to fake left, press Left once then quickly hit Right and drive to the hoop.

💥 You can pop a three-pointer without inbounding the ball. The Birdman is especially good at this tricky move.

💥 Remember, Jordan can make his unstoppable slamma jammas from at least a foul-line's distance away from the hoop. Get open, then press and release button A.

💥 Learn the spin move with both players. When you dribble towards the basket, press B and Down to back against your opponent. Then, when the time's right, quickly press Left (or Right) and then Up to spin around him. Now you're in position to drive or pop a jumper.

💥 Bird's size advantage makes him effective at backing into the basket. Press B and Down to turn his back to Jordan. Then, use the directional pad to back in. You can usually get close enough for an easy turnaround jumper or you can quickly jump back out to the three-point line for three!

💥 Fouling can be an effective defense, and you can't foul out! When your opponent forces you too close to the basket, foul him. He gets a new 24-second clock but he has to inbound from the outside again and you get another chance.

💥 Follow up outside shots so you can grab the rebound if you miss. After you press and release Button A to shoot, immediately use the directional pad to head towards the basket. But don't get too close! Long jumpers have a tendency to bounce long on the rebound.

Of course, it's impossible to keep Larry and Michael from scoring, but smart "D" is critical. Always position yourself between your man and the basket. It ain't easy, but it's the winning difference.

For the best score in the Slam Dunk contest, practice, practice, practice in the Follow the Leader mode. The better you can mimic the computer's dunks step for step, the higher you score.

Timing is the secret in the Three-Point Shootout. Learn to shoot quickly in a smooth rhythm – but move quickly or time runs out before you're done. Be sure to sink the fifth ball from each bin. That's the "money" ball – worth two points!

After you shoot in the Three-Point Contest, don't Press A to grab the next ball until your shot reaches the basket. If you do, the ball disappears in mid-air!

By Tradewest
One to Four Players (simultaneous)

What looks like basketball, plays like basketball, and even sounds like basketball, but isn't exactly basketball? It's Magic Johnson's Fast Break, a cart that offers fast-paced two-on-two basketball action rather than the usual five-on-five contest. On screen you get full-court, horizontally-scrolling gameplay. A referee monitors the action and calls fouls if the gameplay gets too rough, and a fanatical crowd cheers you on.

Your team starts each game at a certain salary level. Your goal is to beat the pants off the opposition to earn a larger salary. Keep winning and you might etch your name onto the Big Earners Screen. Choose from five skill levels – Rookie to Professional. Each level provides quicker gameplay, tougher defense, and bigger bucks if you win.

Each game lasts four three-minute, real-time quarters. In between quarters, you can review stats such as field goal percentage, three-pointers made, rebounds, and steals. If the score is tied at the final buzzer, you play additional quarters until someone wins.

You control one player at a time. An arrow appears on-screen above the head of the player you're running. Just hit B to switch players. You can play against the computer or a friend.

Since there are only four players on screen, there's plenty of room for no-holds-barred, run-and-gun hoops. You'll hear the fans roar and the basketball shoes squeal as players zip up and down the court. And both teams can really rack up the points for radical scoring! So, lace up your sneakers and loosen your fingers – it's time to go for a fast break!

Hot ProTips

💥 Team defense creates turnovers. Learn to double-team the ball handler by pressing B quickly to always keep a player in his face.

💥 Play tight D at midcourt and sometimes you can force your opponent into a backcourt violation.

💥 When you find yourself chasing the ballhandler up court, go for a steal. Pull up along side of him and move into him while rapidly pressing A.

💥 If you dribble the ball upcourt, hug the near sideline. It's almost impossible for the defender to make a steal, and you never step out of bounds.

💥 The draw and kick is a good offensive play. Drive to the hoop, draw the defenders to you, and then kick the ball out to your open man for an uncontested shot.

💥 Computer opponents are quick, so don't try to make a pass when they're near your passing lane or they'll intercept it.

💥 After they score, the computer players are a might slow getting back on D. When you inbound the ball, send a player downcourt off screen. Then press B to pass. (The longer you wait, the closer he gets to the basket, but watch out for a five-second violation.) It's an easy two, if you don't blow the shot.

💥 Fouling as a quarter draws to a close can be a smart defense. You get five team fouls before the other team gets penalty shots and a new quarter wipes the slate clean. Watch the clock and use fouls wisely.

When you commit an offensive foul or a backcourt violation, the other team inbounds the ball. When the scene changes, be ready! One of your players is usually in good position to steal the pass.

 Defensive action underneath your basket gets confusing. On defense pressing B switches players. On offense, it passes the ball. When the other side makes a bucket, you go on offense and one of your players automatically gets ready to make an inbounds pass. Don't press B inadvertently. Your opponent will steal for an easy two.

By Sega of America
One or Two Players (simultaneous)

It's more than appropriate that Pat Riley, former coach of the NBA's Los Angeles Lakers, has his name on a basketball video game that emphasizes the fast break. After all, the LA Lakers play at a frantic pace – slamming, jamming, flying the ball up and down the court in a heartbeat.

Pat Riley Basketball for the Genesis moves at this breakneck pace. The offensive play features half-court passes and slamdunks. In fact, 75% of your shots will be driving layups and dunks. Of course your players can shoot 15-foot jump shots, but that's just too risky when you can dunk the ball unopposed so often.

Good defense can stop a fastbreak offense – so "D" is the key to playing competitive roundball with Pat Riley. Once you master stealing and blocking, the number of dunks by your opponent will drop dramatically.

One or two players choose from eight pro cities such as New York, Boston, Los Angeles, Houston, and Denver. Pick your team and decide whether to play an exhibition or a tournament. Next, select the skill level of the computer opponent: Easy, Normal, or Hard. Teams are fairly even in strength and overall ability, but the five players on the team you choose are all unique. Each one is rated on a scale from one to nine in four categories – shooting, passing, speed, and defense.

Great graphics and some nifty sound effects add to the realism of this game. Once you master the "D," Pat Riley's Slammin' and Jammin' Basketball becomes an exciting, balanced game of roundball – one of the best available for any video game system.

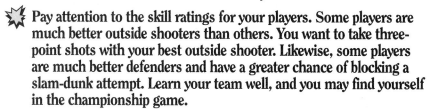

In the Easy and the Normal levels shoot long-range bombs from the backcourt, then position your players under the basket for the rebound and an easy slam dunk.

Pay attention to the skill ratings for your players. Some players are much better outside shooters than others. You want to take three-point shots with your best outside shooter. Likewise, some players are much better defenders and have a greater chance of blocking a slam-dunk attempt. Learn your team well, and you may find yourself in the championship game.

It's important to have a fast player with good passing ability bring the ball up court. With a quick guard you are less likely to have your pass intercepted by the other team or have the ball stolen from behind.

In the Hard level, passing becomes more important because the computer defenders are more aggressive. Pass the ball as soon as a defender gets within reach of your ballhandler.

The "slam-dunk zone" is quite large in this game. Try to shoot as soon as you get the ball into the paint under your opponent's basket. This will almost always become a slam-dunk.

The New York team has the best backcourt in Pat Riley Basketball.

By Aicom/NEC
One or Two Players (simultaneous)

No way a video game compares to real basketball, right? Well, in your face! Takin' It to the Hoop offers all of the excitement, strategy, and action of B-ball for the TurboGrafx-16.

You don't get NBA players, but you may be able to represent your favorite city. You can lead one of eight teams – Honolulu, Seattle, Los Angeles, Dallas, Chicago, Boston, New York, or Miami into tournament, league, or exhibition play. Tournament play features round-robin elimination – you keep playing until you lose or win the tournament! In League play you take on each of the other teams. If you win all the games, you're the champ. The Exhibition mode lets you go head-to-head against one other team in a one-game challenge. Challenge the computer or take on a friend.

You're a player/coach on court, so you'll select the starting five from a 12-man roster and make substitutions throughout the game. You can actually play all five players at once by quickly switching among them. Shoot, dribble, steal, pass, take freethrows, and slam dunk. Individual players are rated on stamina, speed, shooting ability, passing prowess, and defensive skills. You also call the "D." Play zone, man-to-man, or a combination of man and zone.

Hardcore gym rats know there's no substitute for an honest-to-goodness game of hoops. But Takin' It to the Hoop has all the thrills, none of the spills, and some top-notch video roundball. Call time out and give it a try.

🌟 You can win with any team, but some are fundamentally better than others. Miami is the best, with Los Angeles and New York strong seconds. Honolulu plays the best overall defense.

🌟 Most teams have strengths and weaknesses; the challenge is to win with a less balanced team. Frequent substitution is the trick. Study the individual player ratings and tailor your team for the opposition. Also, learn when to make a change. Don't wait for players to tire. Send in the subs if your on-court people are getting the stuff kicked out of them!

🌟 Try bringing the ball upcourt down the wings (the sides) rather than the middle. It's easier for you to see the lanes open up for passes or drives to the hoop.

🌟 If you have a good shooter, get him in the open and keep feeding him the ball.

🌟 Ball hogs get the ball stolen; pass it around.

🌟 Try jump passes. Press Button II and then I.

🌟 If you have a player with Speed rated A, he can pull an exaggerated zigzag move to the hoop, which always loses the man guarding him. You can usually dunk it, if no one else is in position to react.

🌟 Think your starting five can go all the way? Guess again. They slow down when they get tired. Substitute for fatigued players or you'll get blown out.

🌟 To make extremely accurate freethrows, pause the game by pressing Select exactly when the marker reaches the middle of the shooting gauge. Now hold down Button I or II and then hit Select to unpause.

Don't accidentally press Run when anyone's in the closeup free-throw screen. It resets your game.

 You can grab rebounds, so do it!

 Man to man is the best all around defense, it always keeps your players around the ball and makes it hard for the opponent to get a breakaway dunk.

 The best way to steal is to attack from behind.

 Sometimes you can cause a five-second violation and a turnover if you put the defensive player right in the offensive player's face and rapidly press I.

 You can only pass to players you see onscreen.

 Fouling when the score is close and time is tight can be a winning tactic.

CHAPTER 4
Just For Kicks

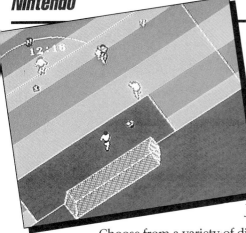

By Jaleco
One or Two Players (simultaneous)

You dribble the ball towards the opponent's goal, pause, and then, with a perfectly timed maneuver, hook the ball to the corner of the net past the goalie! It's soccer at its video game best in Jaleco's Goal!

Choose from a variety of different play options including two-player head-to-head action, World Cup Competition with 16 different teams from around the world, and even a "shoot" contest.

Just as in real soccer, your World Cup and Tournament teams have 11 players. Each team has three forwards, three midfielders, four defenders, and one goalie. Each position has offensive and defensive roles comparable to those of real soccer players. Use the rating charts in the manual to check out each player's skills in the different skill categories like dribbling, kicking power, running speed, tackling ability, shooting ratio, and ball-keeping ability. This helps give you an idea of the overall abilities of the teams.

Once the action starts it's pure soccer. Win by scoring the most goals! Score with hot offense and stop your opponent with tough defense. You'll have all the great soccer moves at your disposal. Dribble the ball downfield, pass it, and shoot it. Put hook, slice, backspin, or longer distance on your shots, head the ball, and tackle it from your opponent.

Standard soccer rules apply, including Goal Kicks, Corner Kicks, Throw-Ins, and penalties – Offsides and Tripping! This is soccer simulation at its best. You'll even hear the roar of the crowd as you race downfield and go for the Goal!

Hot ProTips

⭐ To give yourself the best shot at winning the World Cup, it helps to play with one of the stronger teams! The USSR has the best goalie in the league and a strong defense. England's #10 is the best forward in the league – a skillful shooter who's extremely quick. The USA is a well-balanced team that gets stronger if they get a lead!

⭐ Keep a defender between the goal and the computer's offensive player. If the computer moves past one of your defenders, switch your control to another defender.

⭐ In the second round of play don't waste time passing the ball. By this time in the game the computer defenders are very good, and they'll steal the ball away from you whenever you try to pass it. Move the ball by using the shoot button and slicing or hooking the ball toward your teammates.

⭐ When you get to the finals you'll find that there's no such thing as a tie. In a tie situation the game stages a sudden death shoot-out where you get five chances to score a goal against the computer goalie, and the computer gets a chance to score five goals against you. Whoever makes the most goals wins!

⭐ When your goalie has the ball, pay attention to where the other team's defenders are. Sometimes the other team will try to head the ball into your net when you try to clear it.

Play in the World Cup Finals with any team:

Team	Password
Algeria –	CTXAREZCGPLOPEOB
Argentina –	JTXAREZCGXIKLUEL
Belgium –	ATXAREZCGRHFOEOB
Brazil –	ITXAREZCGPIGKCMB
Denmark –	ITXAREZCGVIGKWIL
England –	JTXAREZCGZLGKUGJ
France –	ETXAREZCGAISKWHJ
Holland –	QTXAREZCGWLUOUGJ
Italy –	DTXAREZCGAHKLUIL
Japan –	PTXAREZCGZMKLWIJ
Poland –	ATXAREZCGUMJPCTD
Spain –	DTXAREZCGOHFOCOB
Uruguay –	ITXAREZCGULGKESB
USA –	HTXAREZCGWHKLWEJ
USSR –	ZTXAREZCGOHGOERB
West Germany –	LTXAREZCGTMGOCRD

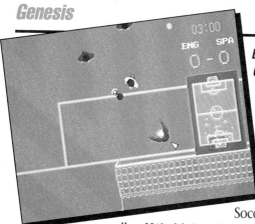

By Sega of America
One or Two Players (simultaneous)

What's the most popular sport in the world today? You lose if you guessed baseball, basketball, football, or even hockey. It's soccer!

World Championship Soccer puts you right in the middle of World Cup Soccer action against 24 teams from around the world. Each game lasts about 15 minutes, so a full tournament takes about an hour and a half. There's no password mode so you've got to play the entire tournament in one sitting. No problem! The thrill of winning the World Cup is well worth the time. There's also a two-player option so you can go head-to-head with a friend to see who takes home the world cup.

Each team is rated from "1" to "5" in four skill categories, with "5" representing the best. The categories are speed, kicking strength, tackling ability, and accuracy. Every player is rated in the same four categories, but each player's scores are based on a comparison with his teammates.

Teams are grouped in zones with four teams playing in each zone. You go up against every team in your zone once, and then the two top teams advance to the final tournament.

When the action begins, you view the field from above. A small radar screen in the upper right corner shows you how close you are to the opposing goal and where other players are on the field.

Dribble downfield, pass to teammates, take a penalty shot, or block a shot at your goal! Whether you're a soccer buff or just a sports fan looking for a fast-paced game, you'll get a kick out of World Championship Soccer.

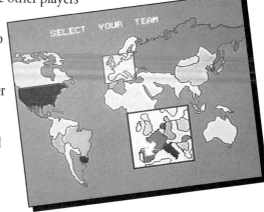

Hot ProTips

⭐ Remember that a player with a "5" in speed playing on a "2" team is not going to be as quick as a player with the same speed rating on a better team.

⭐ You'll probably find the radar screen doesn't help you much. The action in this game is so fast-paced that if you take your eyes off the main screen for even a second, you'll give up a score.

⭐ Don't try to control the tempo of the game by slowing down the pace. You're more likely to catch your opponent's goalie offguard and score more goals if you play at a frenzied pace rather than a slow and meticulous pace.

⭐ The goalie can only move from side to side during regular play. However, during a sudden death shoot out the goalie can dive for a ball.

⭐ Brazil, Argentina, and USSR are the most powerful teams in World Championship Soccer. They are also the most balanced teams.

⭐ Be careful when you choose who starts at what position. On defense try to choose players with high ratings in Tackling Strength and Kicking Power. On offense, Speed and Accuracy are more important.

CHAPTER 5
Racers, Start
Your Engines!

By Data East
One Player

Al Unser Jr. Turbo Racing is an international Formula One tour de force. You race a grueling 16-track World Grand Prix Series in countries such as Brazil, Australia, Monaco, England, Greece, and Japan. All the tracks look the same but each one presents a unique high speed challenge where races last from 6 to 11 laps. Al Unser, Jr. advises you how to tackle each course. Listen to his advice if you want to win.

For every track, you can take solo practice runs or work out against other cars. Then it's a one lap sprint for a qualifying time, which determines your starting position in the 26-car field.

The driving perpective is an NES standard forward-looking, behind-the-car view. Your onscreen display includes Speed, Gear, Lap Time, remaining Turbo power, and Ranking (current field position).

Driving skills you must master include shifting among four speeds including a special Turbo mode and making quick turns. Tight hairpin curves and chicanes abound so this is no flat-out barn burner.

But it takes more than fancy driving to beat the field here. You have to pick the proper time to make your moves. Also, several tracks require you to make time-consuming pitstops for R & R: refueling and repairs.

Your basic goal is to finish in the top six in order to score status points, which you use to customize your car. Ultimately, your total points earn you a spot in the World Grand Prix Championship rankings. Want to join Formula One racing's elite? Put the pedal to the metal with Al Unser Jr. Turbo Racing.

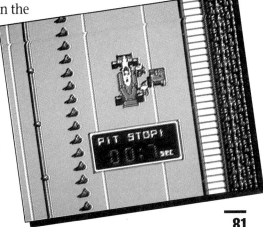

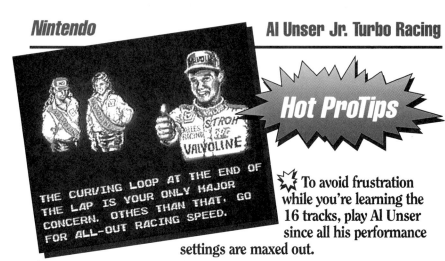

THE CURVING LOOP AT THE END OF THE LAP IS YOUR ONLY MAJOR CONCERN. OTHES THAN THAT, GO FOR ALL-OUT RACING SPEED.

To avoid frustration while you're learning the 16 tracks, play Al Unser since all his performance settings are maxed out.

When you get into customizing your own car, study the tracks. If there are a lot of curves, divvy performance points between Acceleration (ACC) and Suspension (SUS). If there are several straightaways, build up Speed (SPD) and Turbo (TRB). If you're accident prone, you'd better have Durability (DUR) and good Pit Crew Speed (PIT).

The default number of Practice Laps is 99. That's okay as you learn the tracks, but since qualifying times are based on a one-lap sprint, it's better to set Practice Laps to 1 to practice qualifying.

No matter how long it takes, establish a high qualifying time. The further up in the pack you can start the better. In fact, if you're good enough to qualify in the top ten, you should always be able to score points.

If you start back in the pack, be patient. Wait for the traffic in front of you to spread out before you make your moves, or you'll always rear end other cars and spin out.

There are no fiery crashes, but lose it in a turn or bump another car too hard and you'll spin out, which costs you valuable time.

Lay off the brakes unless it's an emergency. Instead, downshift to slow down.

The amount of Turbo speed is limited, so use it wisely. Save it for long straightaways and for making sure-fire passes by other cars. At the end of the race, a burst of Turbo can make a difference of several places in your final standing.

When the Refuel warning flashes, you can last approximately two more laps before you need a pit stop.

 You don't need pit crews for six lap races. You must make pit stops for all other races, but make them quickly, they add to your overall time.

By Acclaim
One or Two Players (simultaneous)

What do you think of when you hear the word "Bigfoot?" Well, if for you the word conjures up images of large, hairy abominable snow monsters, get ready to redefine it in a big way. The only monsters you'll find in this title are of the truck variety. Bigfoot puts you behind the wheel of a monster truck to compete in the monster truck championship of all time.

Here you're pitted against the likes of Greg the Growler as you try to prove just how tough your truck is. To win the tournament you'll have to successfully complete a 4,000 mile rugged trek across the country. Obstacles in the cross-country treks include mud hills, water slicks, car crushes, jumps, and, of course, your monster truck opponent. Along the way you can grab special items like the circular saw and the nitro blast to help you grind your opponent into the dust.

In between the different cross-country treks you'll go head-to-head against other monster trucks in Championship Events. These best two-out-of-three events include car crushing, hill climbing, tractor pulling, and mud running.

Winning events earns you prize money and points towards the championship. Use your cash to stop at auto shops along the way to upgrade your truck or, more likely, rebuild your burned-out engine! You'll also need your cash to pay entry fees at each of the different events. If you're out of cash, you're out of the competition! No problem though! Just put your pedal to the metal and stomp your way to the Bigfoot Championship.

Hot ProTips

⚡ During the cross-country races steer clear of mud and water – they'll really slow you down.

⚡ When you grab the different special items in the cross-country race remember that they don't activate until you hit Button A. Our personal favorite is the Circular Saw. Once you have the saw in place, you'll find that if you hang tough on your opponent's tail, you can actually destroy his truck with the saw.

⚡ Grabbing money during the cross-country race is important but don't forget to score points. Snag money by driving over $ signs and through the checkpoints. Score points by crushing cars along the way.

⚡ If you're low on cash during the cross-country races, drive very carefully. Every time your truck is destroyed by crashing into obstacles like trees, it'll cost you big bucks to put a new truck into action. When you run out of money you're game is over!

⚡ The best way to come across the finish line first at the end of the cross-country race is to save blasts of nitro for the last stretch of hard surface road. A few well-timed blasts usually send you soaring across the finish line in the lead.

⚡ The special Championship Events are tough! If you're up against another player don't even bother to try and shift! Winning comes down to whose thumbs can hit Left and Right faster on the control pad without cramping up! The other key element is making sure you have the correct replacement parts. See the manual for suggested parts for different events, but try to just have four of everything!

⚡ Beating the computer trucks in the Championship events is tough! If you manage to stay close to the computer competitor, your best shot is to try and use a spare finger to hit the Super Charger button. You might just edge across the finish line first.

By Namco/NEC
One or Two Players (simultaneous)

Are you ready to burn some rubber? Well, put your pedal to the metal and climb into Final Lap Twin! Pick between One or Two Player Grand Prix style action or, for a change of pace, head into an unusual racing quest adventure.

In the One Player mode select from practice rounds, "Test," or race to go against the computer in one of two different cars. Pick the F3000 class racers and you battle it out in eight different Grand Prix style races. Climb into an F-1 machine and compete in 16 different races. You've got to finish in the top six in each race to earn points towards becoming the Grand Prix champ. Choose the Two Player racing mode and you and your friend can compete head-to-head for rank in the Grand Prix.

When the green flag drops you'll find yourself roaring around one of twenty different raceways. You control your car's speed, direction, and shifting as you navigate hairpin curves, S-curves, zigzags, and straight-aways. Check your instrument panel to monitor your current rank, lap, rpm's, time, gear, and where you are on the course.

If you're interested in racing action with an adventurous twist, try the Quest Mode! It pits you against a gang of Baby Four-Wheel Drive Warriors. Try to beat them at their own game and become the champ. Journey through a strange land, going one on one against the different drivers you encounter. Beat them and you'll earn prize money that you can use to upgrade your car in the different shops you visit.

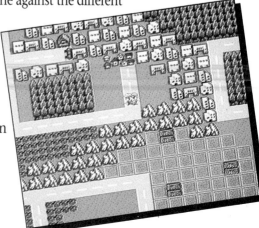

So, whether you like straight-up no-frills racing or an unusual four-wheeled adventure, Final Lap Twin is ready to take you for a ride.

Hot ProTips

⭐ F-1 class cars are faster and have higher powered engines. Start with the F3000 and when you've got some experience move to the higher-powered cars.

⭐ Get some heavy-duty racing under your belt in a car with an automatic transmission before you try the manual shift. It's easy to accidently shift to the wrong gear since the directional pad maneuvers the car and shifts gears. Once you've got a good feel for the handling of the cars on the track you're in better shape to try shifting.

⭐ Practice the tricky hairpin and S-curves to get a feel for the speed and maneuvering needed to successfully navigate those curves. Try taking them tight on the inside corners and letting up on your speed just a little.

⭐ Avoid getting too close to other cars on tight turns. They can force you off of the road.

⭐ In the Quest mode a good starting strategy is to stay near your home town at first. This way you can keep returning to the Practice Track between races to refuel your Turbo while you build up money to buy parts and make your car more powerful.

⭐ To earn a lot of money quickly try to find the little island off the west coast near your home town. There's a really tough girl racer who lives on the island. If you manage to beat her (and you'll need full Turbo to do it), your Dad will give you $3,000.

This password starts you off with a very powerful car. You're ready to find the King and beat him!

> CARR"EV LA"V3Fi
> 1LAAAAA MQLAAG

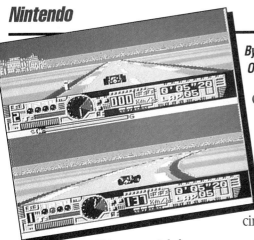

By American Sammy
One or Two Players (simultaneous)

Get ready to jump behind the wheel of one of the sleekest, meanest racing machines ever built – the Formula One. With a little practice you'll earn a shot at being number one on the Grand Prix circuit.

Take your pick from any one of four Formula Ones built for top speed and performance. To make this top-flight racer scream around the track you'll have to master braking, accelerating, steering, and shifting.

World GP lets you take your car for a practice spin on any of the 16 different raceways. Better yet, Michael Andretti himself is only too happy to talk you through the tricky parts of each of the different speedways.

Ready for a real race? Pick your favorite track, grab a buddy, and start your engines. The Two Player Mode pits you against another player or, if there's no one around, a professional driver. There are 13 famous international racers just waiting to match machines with you, including Michael Andretti himself.

To win the coveted title of Grand Prix Champion you'll have to compete in races worldwide and win more points than any of the other racers. This is easier said than done. To enter the Grand Prix you'll have to qualify. If you make it, you'll get a starting position as well as the chance to earn points towards becoming the Champion.

Between the Practice Modes and the variety of cars, raceways, and competition options, there's enough racing action to keep any speed demon busy. So climb behind the wheel of your Nintendo and head for the checkered flag!

Hot ProTips

☆ Beginners should try the standard Ferrari V12. The Honda V10 is great for drivers who haven't mastered manual gear-shifting. For maximum output on long, straight tracks try the Chevy Lola.

☆ To maintain maximum speeds around curves, hold the A and B buttons down simultaneously as you navigate the curve.

☆ Keep off the grass – it does extra damage to your tires.

☆ Time your pit stops based on your tire damage. Go too long without a pit stop and bad tire treads decrease your maximum track speeds.

☆ While you're in the pit stop rapid-fire on the A button will speed up your pit crew. With rapid-fire you can cut as much as 2 or 2.5 seconds off of your pit stop time.

☆ Besides becoming familiar with the tracks, the Practice Mode also gives you a feel for something a little more elementary – shifting! Once your shifting becomes automatic, especially tricky downshifting around tight curves, you'll be much more effective out on the track when you've got other cars to maneuver around.

☆ During the Practice Mode, learn to maneuver around chicanes by running off the track and actually gaining time! Work your speed up to 250 mph, and then, when you come to the chicane, let your car continue straight ahead. If the chicane is a small one, you'll be back on the track with time gained – and nothing more than a slight steering adjustment! Try Monaco on the second straight away and Australia at the first hard chicane to get a feel for this trick.

☆ After you complete each level in the Grand Prix Mode, save the game and return to the Practice Mode for a little warm up on the next Grand Prix track.

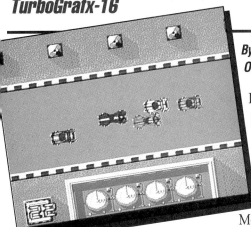

By NCS/NEC
One to Five Players (simultaneous)

Have you ever wondered how people will race in the future? Well, one scenario is that bored with the general peace that reigns across the Earth, the youth of 2015 develop an intriguing sport called Moto Roader. Here's a sporting challenge where skill, strategy, luck, and firepower determine who wins.

Your challenge is to race up to four other players, as well as computer-controlled cars, in an attempt to win prize money and capture the Moto Roader Championship by scoring the most points.

Score points by competing in eight different heats on seven different race courses. Each course is different and some include obstacles such as ramps and buildings. At the end of each heat the racers earn points and prize money based on their finish in that heat. Then it's off to shop for parts to soup-up your car for super speed and power. In addition to the run-of-the-mill parts such as tires, brakes, engines, and bodies, you can also purchase special items. Here's where the racing turns into a futuristic demolition derby. Racers can purchase normal special items like an extra gas tank, or they can grab nifty items like the Hopper (makes your car jump over obstacles), the Warper (warp towards the car ahead of you), and Grenades and Bombs (guess what you do with those!).

As the cars grow more powerful the racing gets wilder, especially in a five-player game. Fasten your seatbelts – it's going to be one bumpy ride!

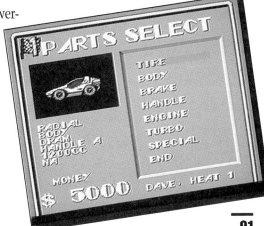

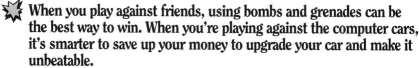

Beginning racers
should always keep an
extra tank of gas. Use it
when your gas meter
reads five or lower.

When you play against friends, using bombs and grenades can be
the best way to win. When you're playing against the computer cars,
it's smarter to save up your money to upgrade your car and make it
unbeatable.

Here's the way our experienced racers like to upgrade their cars:
First, buy a 4800 cc engine, next Body +4, and finally, Bi-Turbo.

If you're nearing the finish line and you're behind, let off on the accelerator so that you're pulled forward, then stomp the accelerator to
speed up.

To check out the Moto Roader tunes in the Sound Test enter either
MUSIC or ART88 on the Entry Board. A menu of tunes comes up
on the screen. Play them by using your control pad.

When you enter the Course Selection Screen, hold the Select button
down, and push the Control Pad to the Right. This activates the
"time" option. At the end of the race you'll be able to check out the
winner's time.

The "slip" option makes your car slip and slide even with the best
tires and brakes. To activate "slip" enter the Course Selection Screen
and push Select and Left on your Control Pad simultaneously.

To begin with $50,000 to spend on parts enter the Course Selection
Screen and push Select and Button II simultaneously. This activates
the "rich" option. You'll have $50,000 to go shopping with. The
computer cars will also have $50,000, but they'll still choose the
cheap parts!

By Nintendo
One Player

Rad Racer is one of the original road race carts for the NES, and it still stands up as a classic today.

Climb behind the wheel of either a 328 Twin Turbo or an FI. The cars perform the same but look different. Your view is from the driver's seat and you can control acceleration, braking, and steering. Hit high speeds and zoom into Turbo-speed to accelerate past the pack.

Rev up your engine and get ready to race through eight different stages in some very exotic locales. For example, you'll zip down the San Francisco Highway, through the Rockies, past the Ruins of Athens, or even across the Grand Canyon. Your goal is to try and complete each course in the alloted time. Sounds simple but you've also got to stay on the road, avoid crashing, and rack up enough kilometers to reset the clock before your time is up.

READER'S TOP 20 CHOICE

Of course this is no Sunday drive. Each of the eight stages has twists, turns, and obstacles along the side of road just waiting for you to smash into. Other unfriendly vehicles, like Corvettes and Lamborghinis, are also out to win the race and they'll try to cut you off or stop you from getting ahead.

It'll take more than just a speed demon to come out ahead in Rad Racer. To win this race it takes a good dose of smarts, skill, and maybe just a little luck to finish in the lead.

⚡ In order to complete any course you must reset the clock by earning points for each kilometer you pass. Don't give up when time runs down and the timer sounds. Squeeze every last kilometer out of your car and you just might reset the clock.

⚡ To continue on the same track you left off on, wait for the demo screen, hold down A, and press Start.

⚡ When traffic bunches up, identify the fastest car in front of you, follow it through the crowd, and whip around it when you're in the clear.

⚡ For turbo speed, press Up while you hold down A (the accelerator). You can kick it in after you reach 100 km/h.

⚡ Learn to dart around cars by "drafting." Get right up behind them by alternately pressing A (accelerator) and B (brake) and quickly make your move when an opportunity presents itself. Learning this move is essential in order to get around the Stage 5 Lamborghini and the Stage 8 Ferrari Testarossa, two notorious road hogs.

⚡ You can make high-speed turns for non-stop turbo running by rear ending the competition on the outside lane at the right moment. For a high speed right turn, hit the car on the left side of the rear bumper with the right side of your front bumper. Vice versa for the high speed lefts. It takes practice!

⚡ Don't ride the brakes into the curves; you'll lose precious time. If you must brake, learn to tap B just enough to hold the turn, then quickly hit A to fly out of the turn.

⚡ Here's how to select your starting level. At the demo screen, press the B button to increase the tachometer indicator by two lights. The first set of two lights indicates Course 1, the next set of two indicates Course 2, and so on up to eight sets for Course 8. To begin at the selected course, hold down Upper Right, press A, and hit Start.

 Want to see the final animated screen sequence? Display the demo screen, push A and Upper Right simultaneously, hit B 60 times, and hit Start.

By Square
One player

If Rad Racer got your motor running, you'll be glad to know that Rad Racer II is more of the same.

Just as in Rad Racer, RR II pits you in a high-speed eight-stage road rally. Within each race you must reach checkpoints within a certain amount of time or you run out of gas. Familiar-looking road hogs and speed demons try to hamper your run.

You don't get to pick your wheels this time around, but that's no sweat since the cars in the original handled the same. Also, your racer's a little tougher; you're more the bang-er than the bang-ee.

The instrument panel sports a high-tech look and houses a road radar, a digital speedometer, a tachometer, a course timer, a lap timer, and a power gauge. In practice you'll concentrate on the radar, which indicates when a turn is coming up and displays an arrow that shows the sharpness of the curve.

The eight stages take you on a transcontinental ride across America. You start in Key West, Florida. Next, Stage 2 is a nighttime drive on the Big Apple expressway. Stage 3, Gettysburg, is a twisting, turning jaunt through a lush valley. But Monument Valley in Stage 4 is a dry desert run. Next, you motor past the nighttime glitz and glitter of Las Vegas in Stage 5. Then, it's up through the snow-capped peaks of Stage 6, the Rocky Mountains. In Stage 7, keep your eyes on the road despite the beautiful Twilight California sunset! Finally, speed across the Bay Bridge, Stage 8, to finish in San Francisco.

With Rad Racer II, the game's the same, only different. But that ain't bad.

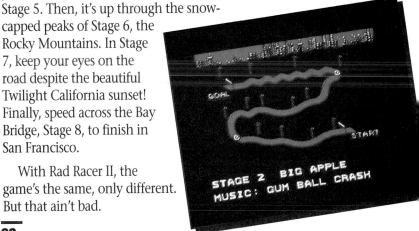

Hot ProTips

☆ You can drive any stage at night by holding down Upper Left and pressing B seven times and then once more for the each successive stage. For example, for Stage 1 press B eight times, Stage 2 press B nine times, Stage 3 press B 10 times, etc. After you select a stage, continue to hold down Upper Left and press Start to begin the game.

☆ To replay a stage, press A and Start simultaneously, then hit Start again to begin the game.

☆ Watch the road radar arrow to cut inside of curves to maintain top speed. That is, when the arrow indicates a sharp left, get to the far left lane and vice-versa for rights. Often, you can use turbo power through the curve.

☆ Whenever the radar arrow points straight ahead, hit turbo even if you're in a curve.

☆ When you cross the shoulder of a road on a turn, don't hit the brakes unless you're about to ram into an obstacle. Ride out the turn and get back onto the road as soon as you can.

☆ If you feel yourself losing it on a curve, release the accelerator (button A) and slide into the turn. Stay off the brakes.

☆ When you enter a curve next to another car, maintain top speed by bumping into it. For a left-hand curve, nose your right front bumper into the left rear bumper of the other car. For a right-hand curve, slam your left front bumper into the right rear bumper of the other car.

☆ If you're up to at least 200 mph at the warning siren, you should make it to the checkpoint.

By Nintendo
One Player

If you like racing action where anything can and does happen, then pull up to R.C. ProAm's starting line for some radio-controlled car racing!

Your NES controller becomes your R.C. controller and in a flash you're maneuvering around the track at top speeds. You'll battle three other cars for the number one spot in 48 different races on 24 different tracks.

Each of the tracks has different obstacles – curves, straightaways, and hazards. Nasty hazards you'll run into along the track include pesky rain squalls, oil slicks that make the track slippery, barriers that pop up to smash your car, skulls who steal your ammo, and mud puddles that really slow you down.

READER'S TOP 20 CHOICE

To contend with all of these obstacles and beat out your opponents, you'll have to grab the Tune-Up items you'll find in different spots on each track. With Turbo for speed boosts, a special engine, and Sticky Tires for great traction, you'll burn up the tracks. Other helpful items to snag include a Roll Cage (to save your neck when your car rolls), and various kinds of ammo, such as bombs and missiles. Use your weapons to bomb an opponent who's right on your tail, or take out the car in the lead!

You begin your racing with a Truck, but grab the letters that spell NINTENDO and you'll find yourself in control of a powerful 4-Wheeler. If you're really hot you might even get to try the Off Roader. This super-cool car is only for the real pros. And we bet you thought radio-controlled cars were only for kids!

Hot ProTips

⭐ As you get set to start a race, hold down B. This gives you a burst of speed at the start that propels you into the lead.

⭐ Look for the red power pads, they'll give you an awesome burst of speed. Learn to hit them consistently. It's the only way to win on some tracks.

⭐ If you lose the pack at night, keep your finger on B, but off the directional pad. You automatically glide around the track and with luck you'll catch the leaders. However, you can't win that way.

⭐ If you spin out or crack up, don't lose your cool. If you straighten out and get back on track fast enough, you usually catch the other cars.

⭐ Until you learn each track, press Start to pause the game before the start of each heat. That way you can study the layout of the track and take off when you're ready.

⭐ Learn to watch slightly ahead of the front of your car. If you observe the track as the screen scrolls you can anticipate the curves better.

⭐ Nice guys finish last. You can bump the competition off the track, but turnabout is fair play.

⭐ It's usually best to hold down B, the accelerator, throughout a race. But for tight hair-pin curves, let up on B for an instant to pivot and then immediately hit it again to power out of the turn.

⭐ You can fire missiles behind you, by purposely hitting an oil slick and firing as you spin around.

⭐ The key to a scoring finish is to complete the circuit without "scraping" the edge of the track. That guides you around curves, but it slows you down considerably.

To make curves at top speed always watch for the yellow arrows and start your turn as soon as you hit them.

 Try to save your armament till the last lap, and the closer to the finish line that you use them the better.

By Sega of America
One Player

You're screaming around a curve, your bike slanted at an impossible angle. Your opponent's just in front of you, trying to run you off the road. With a blast of your turbo you inch past him and blow ahead as he loses traction and goes skidding into a tree. It's custom motorcycle racing of the future. It's Super Hang-On!

The racing is fast and furious in each of the two different modes, Arcade and Original. The Arcade mode is the same great racing you've seen in coin ops. It's pure speed for the thrill of victory. To win you'll have to race across four continents and beat the clock to each of the different check points or you're disqualified. The Original mode was created just for this cart. In it you're a circuit rider. Race against your opponents with your buddy, the mechanic, by your side and a sponsor to fund you. As you win races you'll be able to buy parts to improve your bike and make yourself unbeatable.

The name of the game's the same in each mode. Ride fast, ride hard, and don't wipe out. It takes a combination of skill, nerves, and just plain luck to win.

Additional features that make the game unbeatable include "you are there" 3-D graphics (you'll feel it in every bone when you slam into a tree), four different sound tracks to choose from, and best of all, the ability to build a super bike in the Original mode and then race it in the Arcade mode. Get ready to let it all hang out in Super Hang-On.

Hot ProTips

⚡ To access the Option mode in Super Hang-On hit Button A and Start simultaneously during the title screen. The options you can change include the Game Difficulty (easy to hard) and Time Adjustment (easy to hard). You can also listen to a Sound Test and even change the language of your sponsor, rival, and mechanic to Japanese if you like!

⚡ In the Arcade Mode speed is the key to success since you have to reach each check point before a time limit runs out. In addition, the faster your time in each section, the more time you'll be allotted for the next section.

⚡ In the Original Mode you'll have to drive with a little more finesse. Flat-out speed isn't possible until you've improved your bike with better parts and equipment.

⚡ To keep your speed at its maximum during the Arcade Mode keep your finger on the accelerator. If you need to slow down at all, just lift your finger off the accelerator for a second. Try to avoid using the brakes.

⚡ Improve your speed around corners by cutting your turns close to the inside edge of the curve. But remember that driving on the shoulder of the road slows your speed down quickly.

⚡ Bumping other drivers doesn't gain you anything and slows your speed. Try to navigate around them without touching them.

⚡ Crashing is a disaster in the Arcade Mode. You lose five to six seconds of precious time, and it takes a while to accelerate back up to top speeds. If you see a crash coming, you're better off slowing down.

To see the ending of Super Hang-On try this: after defeating King Arthur in the Original Mode, punch in this password:

> 6FF3F546F35564
> FFOSLPIMFJEDGH

Have the best souped-up motorcycle with the twin turbo from the original mode to play in the Arcade Mode. Just type in this password to see the ending in the Original Mode, but this time select Arcade Mode after punching in the code:

> 6FF3F546F35564
> FFOSLPIMFJEDGH

By Tradewest
One to Four Players (simultaneous)

You may think you know racing, but you won't know racing until you've gone Super Off Road. We're talking trucks, mud, pot holes, ramps, dust, dirt, and sweat. Based on the arcade hit of the same name this classic features four-player simultaneous-action off-road style.

Four trucks compete on each of the eight different tracks with 16 different configurations. That is, race each track clockwise and counter-clockwise. To win you must be the first truck to complete four laps around the track. Sounds easy, but each track is a maze of obstacles including mud, jumps, pot holes, and tons of twists and turns. It isn't easy to maneuver past the obstacles and the other trucks to be the first to bring it on home.

But, hey, if you manage to make it across the line in first place, you earn an extra life and cash prizes. Come in last and you lose a life. Come in last too many times and you'll find yourself gearing up for an early retirement. Use your cash winnings to head for the Speed Shop to buy special accessories such as nitro fuel and better tires. Use these to upgrade your car for the next race.

The first 14 races are the Qualification round, your chance to max up your car for the Tournament. Once you're into the Tournament mode it's an all-out race for the finish as you try to earn enough points to become the Super Off Road champ. Sure it's dusty, dirty, and sweaty, but it's also some hot off-road fun!

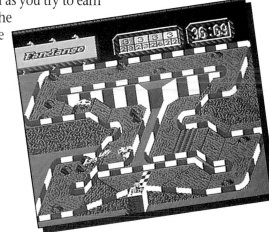

★ If you're taking on the computer don't expect to be a hot shot during your first race. The computer trucks are more powerful and faster than yours. Your best bet is to drive conservatively, go for a decent finish, and then use your money to build up your truck with extra parts after the race.

★ To win at Super Off Road you have to use your Nitro Fuel correctly. Nitro can boost your speed greatly. You begin Super Off Road with a small supply of Nitro so use it carefully during the first race. Keep an eye out for extra Nitro Fuel units that randomly appear on the track. When you buy parts at the end of a race make sure to buy as much Nitro as you can!

★ Although Nitro is key, you'll also need to buy the other four special items to build the overall power and speed of your truck.

★ Nitro speed bursts are most effective on straightaways. Here they'll give you that extra blast to burn by the competition. Nitro fuel can also help you fly over pits and potholes – but just use it to help you take off. Using Nitro while you're in the air is a waste of precious fuel.

★ To navigate around corners without getting out of control try slowing down slightly, tapping the controller quickly in the direction you want to turn, and then accelerating as you come around the corner. Don't use Nitro fuel on the corners. It just gives you too much momentum and sends you flying into the walls.

★ Watch out for puddles and mud holes. Trying to drive through them really slows you down. You're better off avoiding them.

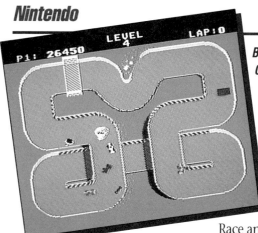

By Tengen
One or Two Players (simultaneous)

If you enjoy life in the fast lane, then get ready to make a Super Sprint for the checkered flag. This arcade classic has made its way into the homes of race fans everywhere.

Race any which way you like. One or Two Players can race on seven different tracks. In fact, the second player can even join a game in progress! Each of the tracks has obstacles ranging from the more mundane, such as hairpin turns and oil slicks, to the exotic, such as tornados and exploding cones.

Once the race begins you've got to complete five grueling laps on each track. Trying to beat you to the finish line are computer-controlled cars and in a Two Player game, your friend. The winner after five laps heads to the next track and a new heat. The losers head for the sidelines! If you win on all seven tracks you begin again on the first track – only this time you'll find new obstacles and tougher opponents.

Your best weapon on each of the different tracks is to drive fast and mean. Hit all of the checkpoints and flags to win points, and collect wrenches to earn the right to customize your mean machine with such nifty extras as Super Traction, Turbo Acceleration, and Higher Top Speed.

Super Sprint's overhead perspective makes for a refreshing "change of race" from other racing titles. Gentlemen, start your engines.

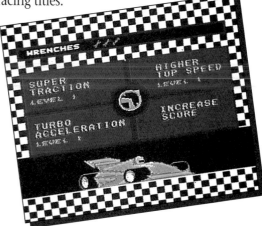

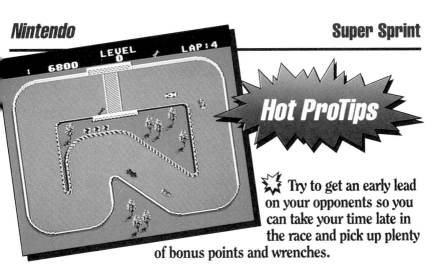

Hot ProTips

⭐ Try to get an early lead on your opponents so you can take your time late in the race and pick up plenty of bonus points and wrenches.

⭐ Get a feel for the rhythm of each individual course. Some tracks have plenty of open straightaways – so you can keep the pedal to the metal. Others have lots of twists and turns, and you must get a feel for when to ease off the gas.

⭐ Use the grass path shortcut at the top of the Level 3 track. It saves you from having to make an extra sharp turn and allows you to gain some ground on the computer opponents.

⭐ The dirt path shortcut on Level 4 (top of the track) turns that part of the track into a great straightaway. Use it to your advantage – the computer-controlled cars won't!

⭐ A Super Traction rating at Level 2 or above is sufficient to prevent you from skidding when you hit water puddles.

⭐ It is important to follow the track in the proper direction. If you skip any portion of the track, you'll have to repeat the entire lap.

⭐ Complete a level in one lap! Using a control pad with a "slow motion" option, activate slow motion as your car is about to complete its first lap. If done properly, you car will be credited for two, three, even five extra laps. If you have only a regular NES control pad, you can perform this trick by hitting the Start button as rapidly as you can as you complete your lap.

By Hudson Soft/NEC
One Player

What takes guts, stamina, courage, and more than a little craziness? How about the Paris-to-Dakar road rally. In this ultimate road race test you must become the perfect union of man and machine as you negotiate one of the most demanding road challenges ever devised.

The road rally is not your average round and round race. You'll have to drive your vehicle across continents through varied conditions, night and day, where anything can happen. Your basic challenge is to complete the

13,000 kilometer course, and complete it faster than any of the other drivers. The race itself consists of eight different stages, from the rolling hills and hairpin turns of the French countryside to the grueling desert conditions of the Sahara. Finish each stage in a set amount of time or less to advance to the next stage and earn reserve time for later, tougher stages.

Maneuvering your vehicle across the countryside isn't your only challenge. You'll also have to maintain it by performing repairs and adding replacement parts as necessary. Monitor your car's condition by keeping an eye on your dashboard which indicates your speed, position, gear, wear and tear on your parts, stage number, and time. Learn to shift gears, handle different road conditions, and generally drive smart and fast.

If you make it to the finish line, you'll have the satisfaction of knowing that you've completed one of the toughest road challenges around. Even better, finish in record time and you'll rank right up there with the pros. Maybe you'll even be number one when you make your Victory Run!

Hot ProTips

⭐ During the first two races you'll have 20 points to allocate between the different support parts of your car. Try allocating your points as follows:

Engine:	At least eight points.
Tires:	At least four points.
Gear:	Four points.
Brakes:	Two points.
Suspension:	Two points.

⭐ You don't have to play the speed demon to win in this game. Let off on the gas while attempting to turn. Very sharp turns such as hairpin curves require braking.

⭐ In later stages of the game you'll find yourself driving through hilly areas. A stronger suspension comes in handy here because it's tough on your car when you rocket over the tops of the hills.

⭐ For areas with dirt- or ice-covered roads you'll need to beef up your tires.

⭐ Watch out for cars that come up from behind you when you're slowing down for curves. If they smash into you, they can cause you to spin out or fly off the road.

⭐ When you crash, downshift quickly to ensure a fast recovery.

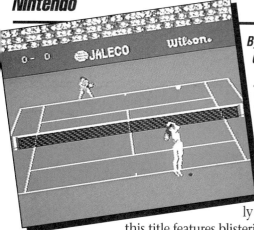

By Jaleco
One or Two Players (simultaneous)

Tennis anyone? Well, slip into your tennis togs, grab your racket, and head for the courts. For gamers who love the ever-popular sport of tennis Jaleco's Racket Attack is a must. Designed to accurately simulate the sport of tennis, this title features blistering on-court action that's hard to beat – but we know you'll give it your best shot!

In Racket Attack you choose between two different modes of play. One Player tennis drops you right into the middle of a national tennis tournament. Win seven increasingly difficult matches and you'll take home the championship trophy. Two Player tennis puts you on opposite sides of the net, hitting it out in head-to-head singles action.

Once you've selected your mode of play decide between men's and women's tennis and choose from eight players in each category. Each of the eight different men and women players has different strengths and weaknesses. For example, among the men, Carter has a great lob shot and a mean passing shot, while Horn has a powerful serve. The women netters include Berry who has powerful top spin but no stamina, and McKay who has great serves and dynamite net play. Check your manual for the rundown on each and every player.

Once you've picked your player, it's time to select your court surface. The game features hard, clay, and grass courts. Then it's time to serve it up. Play follows the regular rules of tennis. Win your match by winning two out of three sets. It's simply smashing!

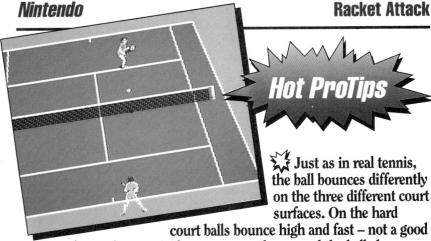

Just as in real tennis, the ball bounces differently on the three different court surfaces. On the hard court balls bounce high and fast – not a good surface to learn on! Clay courts are slower, and the balls bounce lower. This is a good court to learn on, but watch out for slices and short shots. They can be difficult to return unless you're speedy. Grass courts are the most unpredictable. The ball may really take off after it bounces. Remember, Wimbledon is played on grass, so try this surface when you're a pro!

To serve, toss the ball with the B button and then after the ball reaches the top of the toss, just as it starts to drop, hit the A button. Once you've mastered the flat serve, put some spin or slice on the ball by hitting Left (spin) or Right (slice) on the control pad just before you hit the A button.

The first challenge in Racket Attack is to master the timing of your swing and actually hit the ball! You must be in just the right spot, not too far in front of or behind the ball, and you've got to hit it at just the right moment. This means you must MOVE! Don't wait for the ball to come to you; go for it! For groundstrokes, try to get within a racket's length of the ball and swing just after the ball bounces.

Once you've got the hang of returning the ball you can vary your shots. If you hit the ball as it is to your right or left, you'll return it straight back. Hit the ball when it's just past you, and you'll angle your shot to the right. Hit the ball when it's in front of your body, and you'll angle it to the left. Use normal tennis strategies. If your opponent is to your left, hit the ball to the right!

If your opponent hits the ball short, come into the net to volley. Volleying is pretty easy to control in Racket Attack. Use the B button to lob and volley and the A button to smash. The smash is the hardest shot for your opponent to return. Angle your volleys using the same timing as you use for groundstrokes. Great net play is often a winning strategy.

Use these passwords to play each of the second through seventh matches on the way to the championship as First:

2nd Match:	JSLPVYC
3rd Match:	GKVYLWC
4th Match:	PSFRCHC
5th Match:	KYIMYDD
6th Match:	IXKOWCD
7th Match:	RYTONMD

Championship Passwords for Each Player and Each Court Surface:

Player	Hard Court	Clay Court	Grass Court
Bernard	YIBDEPB	GOVWKXC	UVOPSND
Watt	FLYDAYB	KBINXFC	OWERDKC
Carter	KBIQWHC	LAJRWJC	QASROPE
Gibbco	BPDWCSP	RYTNMKD	YIBEGSB
First	OWEQBHC	WXMPTQD	EMXBJYB
Horn	PVFUALC	CSAXGYB	FLYFIDC
Eagle	PVFWANC	NTHYYMD	RYTTNRD
Brofsky	VUPUPQD	YIBHFUB	XWNSTUD
McKay	DRBIEIB	GOVLKMC	QASAOXB
Jansco	TBRANAC	TBRAOBC	FLYPINC
Berry	UVOAQVC	NTHCYPC	EMXJJHC
James	VUPCPXC	IYKXVLD	UVOBSYC
Orchler	YIBMEYB	YIBMFAC	FLYJIHC
Juana	VUPEPAD	SCQWPXC	SCQWQYC
Spohn	CSAFFFB	MUGDAQB	QASXOVC
Gray	CSABFBB	GOVFKGC	EMXHJFC

By Asmik
One to Four Players (simultaneous)

The Australian Open, the French Open, Wimbledon, and the U.S. Open – the biggest names in tennis compete in these tournaments every year trying to win the coveted Grand Slam. So, why not you? Well, now there's nothing in your way. Asmik's Top Players' Tennis lets you compete for the Grand Slam right along with the pros.

Choose from many different play modes – Singles (against the computer or another player), Doubles, and even One Player vs. Two Players on the other side of the net! In the Singles mode you head out on tour with the choice of slipping into the tennis togs of Chris Evert or Ivan Lendl or developing your own tournament player. If you decide to go it alone, you'll allocate points among different skills – speed, stamina, strength, agility, concentration, technique, and even miracle shot ability. Compete in the Asmik Open and try to win enough qualifying matches to rank high enough to play in the Grand Slam Tournaments. As you win matches your player earns points and becomes stronger in the different skill levels. A password mode enables you to hang tough with the same player through thick and thin.

If you've got a friend, or even three, in the mood for a set or two there's a game here for you. Play Singles against one another, or play Doubles on your own, or with up to three friends using the Nintendo Satellite. In Doubles play you'll head straight to the Grand Slam tournaments. What's more, Evert or Lendl are always ready to team up with you for some great doubles action. You'll be standing on center court at Wimbledon before you know it!

⭐ Evert and Lendl's abilities are based on their tennis skills in real life. For example, Lendl has a blistering serve, and Evert is strong and steady from the baseline with lots of stamina. Evert and Lendl are also available for advice during a tough match.

⭐ Choose Evert or Lendl for the first few practice matches. Once you've gotten a feel for their different special skills you can check out how they're allocated. This gives you a better idea as to how you'll want to allocate your special skill points when you develop your own player. For example, you might want your player to have tons of stamina or lightning-fast speed, as opposed to strength or agility.

⭐ Every player you're up against in the Singles Mode has different strengths and weaknesses. During the first few games of a match play conservatively, staying back on the baseline until you've assessed your opponent's gameplay. Once you've found their weaknesses you can adapt your play style and go after them aggressively. For example, if a player is not particularly fast, run them from side to side and, before you know it, they'll miss the ball!

⭐ Overall, the same strategies that work in real tennis work in Top Players' Tennis. If your opponent runs to the net, drill a shot down the sideline or hit a sharp crosscourt angled to pass your opponent clean! Or, toss a lob right over his head! The game includes a complete set of tennis rules, and the rules are the same as in the real game.

⭐ Unless you're really quick, it's easier to stay back at the baseline. You've got a lot more time to get into position and hit the ball. When you're up at the net, just as in real tennis, things happen very fast!

⭐ The timing of your swing is the key to great serving. Swing just as the ball begins to drop back down towards you. Once you've got the timing down you can serve the ball fast or slow, and even put some spin on it.

Mix up your shots. In addition to normal flat groundstrokes, volleys, and smashes, you have the ability to use your controller to put top spin, side spin, and a little slice on your shots.

 Miracle Shots don't work well until you've earned enough Miracle Points! As you gain skill and experience you'll gain the ability to make impossible shots just like the pros, including the Miracle Return (you don't even have to touch the ball), the Miracle Spiral (twists and turns to totally confuse your opponent), and Miracle Speed (a blazing shot that leaves your opponent gasping in disbelief).

Try the finals of the French Open – your're Lendl, battling Evert:

```
D?AA! GNLAN YABLL
JDLZU UC♀4L NIHGU
KVDQP YOIEL L♂HRE
```

Try the first round of the U.S. Open as Lendl:

```
DYAA! GNL7N YEBLL
JKLLU QC♀NL NI!GX
QBDCF KOIEL LKHME
```

By Namco/NEC
One or Two Players (simultaneous)

It's 40-30 and match point. Win this point and victory is yours. You toss the ball and smash the serve – it's an ace! Turbocharged tennis? You bet!

Whether you're on your own or you have a crowd of friends ready for a match, there's a play mode for you. In World Court Tennis you can play Singles or Doubles. In Singles play, you can play the computer or a friend. Play Doubles with up to three friends at once!

Pick your game mode and then select your player. There are 18 different players to choose from, each with a wide range of play skills. For instance, Smith is a lefty who doesn't put any spin on his strokes. If you play against the computer, you also select your computer opponents.

Once you've picked your player, select a court. Choose hard, grass, or clay court surfaces. You can also choose between a one-set winner-take-all match or a two-out-of-three-set match. When your match begins it's up to you to serve, stroke, volley, and smash your way to glory.

But you say you're bored with normal tennis action? World Court Tennis also lets you head out on a tennis quest. An evil King has taken over the land and won't let anyone play tennis. Ace that you are, you're going to beat his evil minions in a series of one-game tennis matches. You can earn prizes, buy special tennis equipment, and eventually take on the evil King himself in a match to end all matches.

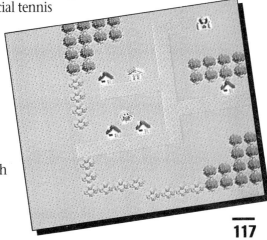

This tennis cart combines top-notch Singles and Doubles action with the whimsy of an unusual tennis adventure. It's game, set, and match for World Court Tennis.

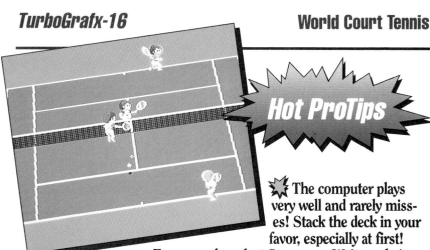

Hot ProTips

⚡ The computer plays very well and rarely misses! Stack the deck in your favor, especially at first! For example, select Stevens or Weitz and pit yourself against a player like Davis. When you get the hang of the game, match yourself against the tougher pros.

⚡ The clay court is the slowest, easiest-to-control surface. On grass the ball doesn't bounce as much, and the hard court is the fastest and the liveliest. Clay is your best choice until you've got the timing of your shots down.

⚡ If you're having trouble with double faults on your serve, check the timing of your swing. If the ball's going long, let it drop a little more before you hit it. If your serve is going into the net, you're letting the ball drop too low before you hit it.

⚡ When you're receiving from a player with a weak serve, move in to "no man's land" so you can blast the serve back cross court or down the line to catch your opponent off guard.

⚡ If you're a player with good volleying skills, head to the net as quickly as possible. Volleying puts you in command, especially when you're on the near side of the net.

⚡ You'll miss your overhead smash unless you're in exactly the correct position. If you have problems with this shot, it's much safer to let the ball bounce and return it with a normal ground stroke.

Try this password for the Quest mode. You've got the Magic Ball, the Inner Tube, Shirt A, RAcket A, and Shoes A. Now go get the Tennis King!

Q♪OdKICAFFFP⛄P♥

By Sega of America
One or Two Players

The din of the crowd quiets to a hush as you approach the ball. You're only two strokes off the leader's pace with three holes left to play. Read the green properly, and you'll birdie this hole. So goes Arnold Palmer Tournament Golf, one of the most realistic and graphically stunning golf games you'll ever play.

Select your level of play, and then head for the pro shop to choose between Black Carbon, Glass Fiber, and Super Ceramic Clubs.

Tee off by yourself or play 18 holes with a friend. Besides the One and Two Player modes there's also a practice mode, match play (head to head), and a full-blown international tournament, where you'll stroke it out against 15 tough competitors.

Tournament play lasts 12 rounds, 18 holes of golf each. Most rounds are standard "stroke" play but the seventh and eighth rounds are "match" games. Things get really exciting when a match game ends in a tie, and players move into a sudden death play-off.

During the tournament players earn higher skill levels, more knowledgeable caddies, and more power. You'll earn a password at the end of each round of the tournament.

Arnold Palmer Golf nets you starting times on three different courses; Japan, the United States, and Great Britain. Golf enthusiasts and newcomers alike will thrill to the excitement of a clapping and cheering crowd when they sink a putt. This game scores a hole in one!

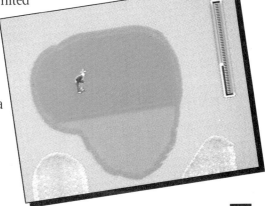

Hot ProTips

⭐ The Japan course is 6,690 yards – a short course surrounded by a water hazard and woods. The United States course is 6,919 yards, wide, and often very windy. Great Britain's course is filled with thick bushes and plenty of sand traps. It's the longest course at 6,950 yards. All three courses are par 72.

⭐ Get a good lie on the fairway and you can try something you'd never do in real golf – hit your second shot with the driver! Since the driver's rated for a longer distance than any other club, it really sends the ball for a ride.

⭐ Don't ignore the wind gauge, wind always affects your shots.

⭐ Remember, it takes three button presses to hit the ball, but you don't have to complete a shot that doesn't feel right. There's no penalty for starting again.

⭐ The computer always lines up your shots directly at the flag. Of course, that means your second shot might be aimed directly at a bunker or over an impossibly long body of water. Look for landmarks in forward view and check them against the overhead screen to see what type of terrain you're hitting into.

⭐ Use the club distance ratings in the manual, that's why they're there! But when you judge the distance for your final approach shot, remember that the ball bounces forward once it hits anywhere on or near the green.

⭐ Mastering the putting gauge is a challenge, but halfway up is usually good for approximately ten yards.

⭐ Generally, the computer lines up the putts correctly.

When you're in the rough, but you have a good lie within 15 feet of the cup, try using the putter for greater accuracy.

When you land in the bushes, take a drop or hit again. You'll never blast your way out of there.

If a tree blocks your way, don't panic. They often appear closer than they actually are. Even if it looks impossible, you can usually hit the ball over them.

If your ball gets buried in a bunker, don't go by the book. Unless you have a good lie, always hit the ball harder than the club distance rating in the manual.

Your caddy has valuable information regarding the way wind direction affects hitting distances that will guide your club selection. When the weather vane appears as you prepare your shot, press C and then A to ask him for advice.

Here are some Passwords so you can jump to other levels in Arnold Palmer Tournament Golf:

This password enables you to play Round 6 head-to-head match play as the champion with $340,000, Power 7, Skill 7, and Caddy Level 4:

> ElA+ CpJ0 KAFU 7BEU
> VAqC RGSW pk4E goL8
> LrHo

This password enables you to begin Round 8 as the tournament leader with $348,000, Power 7, Skill 7, and Caddy Level 4.

> B1J- Pyo3 IIFA vUQ4
> aPCC RCao SU8E goUI
> a4TO

Here's a password for Round 9 that will really help you improve your tournament-leading scores by boosting you to Skill 8, Power 7, Caddy Level 4, and $358,000.

> BhMu +TI- qCBR +g0L
> KdIK SWK5 W44A EIY7
> XxWa

Round 10 is the second Match Play round. This password not only improves your Power and Skill levels, but also enables you to start play as a formidable second tier winner – $372,000, Power 8, Skill 9, and Caddy Level 4.

> F1fp 5+D3 CCEE -08D
> KXIg TC6e GJIQ NJEQ
> RFXC

By Bandai
One or Two Players

Great golfers everywhere look forward to the chance to play 18 holes on one of the most famous courses in the world, Pebble Beach. Now you can play on this challenging course anytime you like. Just plug in your nearest NES and get ready to tee off.

One or Two Players can play a round on this video course modeled after the real Pebble Beach. Each player can select their own handicap. Every one of the 18 holes has the familiar golf hazards – bunkers, slopes, and water hazards. You'll also have to contend with some of Mother Nature's hazards like changing wind conditions and Pebble Beach's most difficult obstacle – the ocean!

Once you tee off you'll have all kinds of decisions to make. Check your score card to see how you're doing. The card also tells you the distance in yards and par for each hole. The computer gives you a bird's-eye and cross-sectional view of each hole, as well as close-ups of the green. You select the right club for each shot. Control your shot to get the power, distance, and hook or slice you want on the ball.

After you've made your shot the computer tells you what kind of a lie you have as well the remaining distance to the hole. Whether you're ready to putt it in or chip out of the bunker it's great golf. All that's missing is the golf cart!

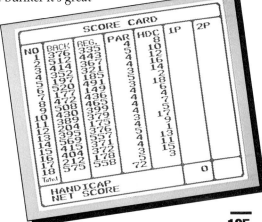

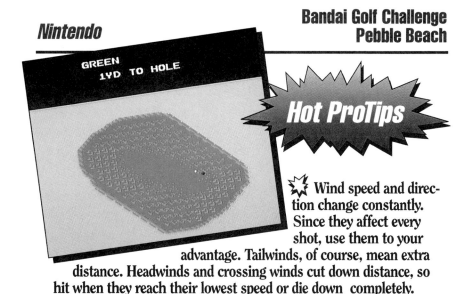

GREEN
1YD TO HOLE

Hot ProTips

⭐ Wind speed and direction change constantly. Since they affect every shot, use them to your advantage. Tailwinds, of course, mean extra distance. Headwinds and crossing winds cut down distance, so hit when they reach their lowest speed or die down completely.

⭐ To a certain degree you can select wind speed and direction for your shots. You have to press A twice to set up a shot. So, press A once, pick your club, line up the shot. Don't hit A again, until you see a setting on the wind gauge that you like. Now press A and you take the shot with that wind speed and direction.

⭐ To beat the 7th hole's stiff headwind for a chance at a birdie, tee off with the four iron and wait for the headwind to change to a crossing breeze.

⭐ The computer usually sets up a decent tee shot except for the10th, the 14th, the 16th, and the 18th holes. Examine the hole and adjust your aim accordingly.

⭐ On the 16th hole the computer aims your tee shot over water. You can play it safe and aim away from the water, but for the maximum distance, press Right once. You'll just make it over the water onto the fairway. Don't slice.

⭐ The only way to keep scores low is to master the short game (pitching wedge and sand wedge) and putting.

⭐ The pitching wedge and the sand wedge are good for approximately 80 yards at full contact.

⭐ Knowing the distance to the hole before each shot is essential to learning how to choose clubs – especially since there are no written distance ratings for clubs. The computer displays distance to the hole after every shot but only once. Don't press A too quickly after you hit or the distance figure vanishes – and you can't re-display it.

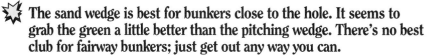 The sand wedge is best for bunkers close to the hole. It seems to grab the green a little better than the pitching wedge. There's no best club for fairway bunkers; just get out any way you can.

The pitching wedge is always better than the sand wedge for chip shots from 25 – 10 yards out.

Chip shots roll, especially when they hit the green. Try to cut approximately five yards off your distance calculations when you go for the flag.

Don't complete shots or putts that aren't exactly right. It's always a mistake. Just refrain from making the final button press to make any shot a practice stroke.

By Konami
One to Four Players

Hey, how about a round or two of golf with the Golden Bear, Mr. Nicklaus himself! And as long as you're gonna play, how about playing on some of the greatest courses around – Pebble Beach, Augusta, Royal Lytham, St. Andrews and more? An impossible dream? Nope, with Jack Nicklaus's Greatest 18 Holes of Major Championship Golf you can do all of the above – if you ever finish saying the name!

One to four players can line up to tee off for a round of 18, Skins or Stroke play. If you need some computer players to round out your four-some, pick from eight, including Jack N and others, each with different golf games.

Each of the 18 holes of this video course are modeled after different holes from famous courses throughout the world.

Once you're ready to tee off pick your club, aim your shot, and use the power bar to determine the distance and angle of your shot – right down to the hook and slice on the ball. You'll have to contend with all kinds of hazards at each hole including wind, bunkers, and water. When you get to the green you'll have to read it and putt the ball into the hole.

Whether you're a hacker or a pro, Jack Nicklaus's golf has a course that fits your style. Jack Nicklaus was voted Golfer of the Century, and this cart (no pun intended) may just follow in his footsteps.

Hot ProTips

Never assume the computer lines up putts correctly.

If you want to skip the intro screens at the beginning of each hole, press B after you sink your putt to go directly to the tee.

You don't need to compensate very much for the wind, but any time you get a tailwind from the tee, wack the ball!

There are no breaks in the green, but when you line up your putts, you must aim slightly to the right of the hole.

Golfers use their putters to help them line up putts; you can use your NES controller to make your putts more precise. Flip the controller 90 degrees so that Right points up. Now place the controller's right edge against the TV, lined up with the hole. Use the direction pad to move the putt marker and use the edge of the controller to help you line up the putt. Sounds hokey, but until you learn to eye-ball putts, it's very accurate.

Overswing from the tee on every hole but the 14th.

On the 14th hole, it's approximately 300 yards from the tee to the middle of the first massive sand trap. Don't overswing here.

Overswinging just takes two button presses. When the bar hits the top of the Power Bar, it automatically starts back down.

You can't miss putts of three feet or less as long as you make the second press quickly.

The 1st hole (#8 at Pebble Beach) is 442 yards. Jack can't clear the water straight to the flag, but he can cut the corner pretty cleanly for a good second shot. Aim for the tiny light patch of ground near the top of the screen, the small tip of land to the left at the edge of the water. It's 312 yards away; overswing and you'll hit it dead on.

By SNK
One to Four Players

Climb into your favorite golf cart and motor down to the first tee. You're invited to join famous golf pro Lee Trevino in a round of golf.

Pick between two different 18 hole courses, one in the USA and one in Japan. In Stroke Play you can tee off with up to three friends. In the Nassau Mode you play against the computer. If your golf game is a little rusty, the Practice Mode enables you to brush up your skills on any hole you'd like.

Slip on your favorite plaid knickers and become one of four golfers – Pretty Amy, Big Jumbo, Super Mex (Lee Trevino), or Miracle Chosuke. Each of the golfers plays a different game. You'll have to play as each of them to see whose golf shoes fit you most comfortably.

When you step up to the tee you'll have to do more than just hit the ball. Check the green, wind speed and direction, and how far you are from the hole. Choose your club, although your caddie is glad to make a recommendation if you're not sure. Whether you're driving down the fairway or lining up a putt on the green, you'll have to aim the ball yourself. You can hook or slice the ball as well as determine the power of your shot.

Every hole on each of the two courses is different. From bunkers to water to roughs and the woods, there are more obstacles than you can shake a golf club at. But don't wrap your favorite putter around a tree. This is the kind of challenge that golf fans everywhere will enjoy.

OUT 2
373Y
PAR 4

SUPER DEEP
ROUGH AT
RIGHT SIDE
OF FAIRWAY
AND GREEN.
KEEP SHOTS
STRAIGHT.

Hot ProTips

The graphics for boundaries are imprecise, so don't hit balls too close to hazards. Land too near the edge of water or O.B., for example, and you're in, even though it doesn't appear that way onscreen.

Of course, Super Mex is the best all-around player if you can master his fairly quick swing.

Practice, practice, practice before you challenge the computer in a Nassau. It's deadly.

Don't trust the computer to line up tee shots, long fairway shots, or long putts correctly. Always check the terrain.

The wind isn't a major factor, but always take it into account when you need a precise shot such as hitting towards hazardous terrain or when you're lining up a critical short iron shot.

Avoid inadvertent button presses. Once you start a swing you must complete it. No second chances here.

All shots take a big bounce and roll, so play shots a few feet short.

Press B to display the crosshair to line up shots. Use the directional pad to extend the crosshair towards the target. Pretty Amy and Miracle Chosuke have the longest targeting distance: sometimes you can place the crosshair right on the hole – a real advantage.

Pretty Amy and Miracle Chosuke have average power, but they're easy to control and consequently very accurate, especially for beginning players.

When you're learning to play with Super Mex and Big Jumbo, try using the sand wedge and the putter for chip-shot accuracy. The sand wedge has better backspin then the pitching wedge up close;

use it from 10 to 15 feet out. Under 10 feet on light rough use the putter.

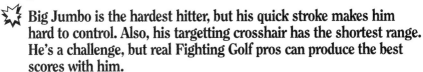 Big Jumbo is the hardest hitter, but his quick stroke makes him hard to control. Also, his targetting crosshair has the shortest range. He's a challenge, but real Fighting Golf pros can produce the best scores with him.

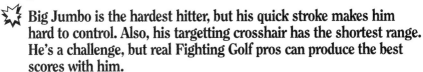 The trees are vicious here. Avoid them as much as possible.

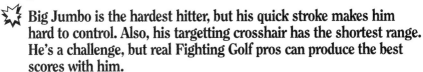 With Super Mex and Big Jumbo, putts from three feet out and closer are a challenge because you must press A two times extremely quickly. Consider playing for longer putts four to seven feet out to give you more time.

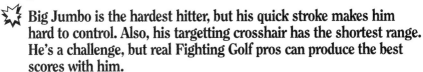 You can use the one wood for extra distance, but your ball must be on the fairway.

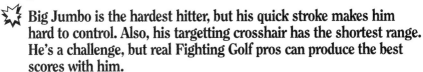 Until you develop a feel for putting distances, use the Club display box to measure your stroke. From five to seven feet out make your second press when the power line hits the right edge of the box. For 10 to 15 feet putts aim for the shaft of the "T" in "PT." From 22 to 25 feet out aim for the shaft of the "P" in "PT."

By Hudson Soft/NEC
One to Three Players

You're teed-up at the 18th Hole. A par here and you finally beat the course record. You make your draw and clobber the ball! It's a beautiful shot – right into the water! Welcome to the all-too-real world of Power Golf!

Power Golf provides 18 holes of horizontally-scrolling golf on a tough video course. You get three types of games: Stroke Play, Match Play, and a long-ball driving contest and closest-to-the-hole competition.

Competition enables three golfers to play simultaneously as one of three different characters. Player One uses a medium-speed swing for a balance of power and precision. Player Two's unhurried, smooth swing and average power produce great accuracy. Player Three has a quick stroke that's hard to master, but you can really send the ball for a ride. Mix players or use clones of the same player.

Once you're ready to tee off, use the direction key to aim an onscreen arrow to line up your shots. A distance chart helps you make smart club selections, taking the wind and other conditions into account. As you start to swing a window pops open for a vertical view of the fairway from behind your golfer as he addresses the ball. Use the power meter to guide your stroke, but watch out for slices and hooks.

Putting's easier, but you've got to read the green's slope, angle, and distance for a perfect shot.

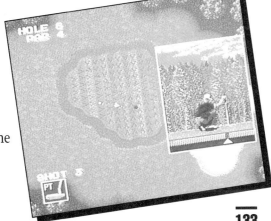

You better stop reading and reserve a tee-off time. If golf's your game, this cart is guaranteed to get you into the swing of things.

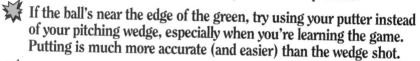

Hot ProTips

⚡ To quickly learn the game, try Match Play versus the computer. Use the same player as the computer. That way, you can observe the computer player's game and use your clone to practice.

⚡ If the ball's near the edge of the green, try using your putter instead of your pitching wedge, especially when you're learning the game. Putting is much more accurate (and easier) than the wedge shot.

⚡ When the hard-hitting Player Three makes a good hit, the ball almost always travels a full club farther than the ratings chart indicates. For example, if you're 179 yards away and the chart calls for a hard four iron, try to nail a five iron instead for better accuracy.

⚡ If you get a good lie on the long fairway, most real-life golfers use a three or a four wood. Use the driver instead and power up for a few extra yards. Player Three is especially good at this.

⚡ Trees are a mean obstacle, but you can hit under them or over them. Smack the ball and immediately press the direction key up to make your shot take a low trajectory; press the key down to loft a high shot.

⚡ The seventh hole is an aquatic nightmare – three islands and water everywhere! Don't try to be cute. Go for it with your driver. Odds are you'll end up in the drink, but for the best score, take the penalty and keep playing. If you're lucky, the ball skips across the water.

⚡ On the 18th Hole, only the long-driving Player Three has a chance of clearing the first bushy hazard from the tee. All others should play less club, a five or a six iron is a good choice. Then use a wood for a strong second shot.

By Electronic Arts
One player

Most so-called "martial arts" carts may be entertaining beat-em-up games, but they don't depict real martial arts. Budokan combines great game-play with a true-to-life portrayal of classic Okinawan Karate and Japanese Kendo.

Your task is straightforward: Master four martial arts well enough to represent the Tobiko-Ryu Dojo with honor at an all-star tournament in Tokyo's Budokan. You learn Karate, Kendo, and classic karate weapons the Bo (long staff) and the Nunchaku (double clubs). Of course, you can skip class and go directly to the Budokan, but bring along plenty of Band-aids.

Practice by yourself or face-off against a computer opponent with three degrees of skill. The moves are intricate and numerous; Karate alone has 31 possible actions. Visit the Free-Spar Mat to practice your skills against any other fighting form, for example, Karate versus Kendo. This is also the only place where you can play another person.

At the Budokan you face 12 opponents, who are experts of rare martial arts forms as well as different styles of the ones you know. For example, you'll face masters of the Tonfa (double sticks), the Kusari-gama (sickle and chain), and the Naginata (long lance) – all classic Okinawan and Japanese weapons.

Budokan accurately portrays martial arts in a sophisticated, almost elegant way. Even the manual is well-done. Here's a martial arts cart that emphasizes the "art" over the "martial" without scrimping on the action.

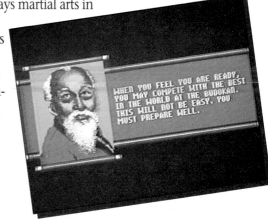

Hot ProTips

⚡ You need room to maneuver. Don't let an opponent force you to the edge of the mat. When the match begins quickly advance to the center of the mat and fight from there.

⚡ Resting builds Stamina, but if you hold a block Stamina doesn't increase.

⚡ If your stamina is almost exhausted, don't waste energy by moving or jumping. Build it up or you're finished.

⚡ Always watch your opponent's Stamina level. If it's lower than yours, attack.

⚡ Fighting with Karate, Kendo, and the Bo you repeat strikes each time you press a button. But with the Nunchaku, just hold the button down for lightning quick multiple strikes.

⚡ Karate's High Block (press Upper Left Diagonal and a button simultaneously) is very strong defense against the Nunchaku.

⚡ Karate's Crouch Sweep Kick is a very effective inside move. Press Down, then simultaneously hit Lower Left Diagonal and a button. For multiple sweeps, keep the button pressed down.

⚡ Longer is better. The weapons in order according to length and effectiveness are: the Bo, the Nunchaku, and the Kendo shinai (bamboo sword).

⚡ The Bo is your best weapon. However, to win at the Budokan, you must also learn to defeat it.

⚡ The Bo's Mid Block is very effective against the Kusari-gama (sickle and chain).

☆ Learn the lower spin moves for Karate and the Bo, no one can defend against them. But stay alert, your opponents try to counter quickly with low blows.

☆ The forward jump strikes in Karate and Kendo (simultaneously press Upper Right Diagonal and any button) are their most powerful moves. But they eat a lot of Stamina.

☆ You can press all three buttons at once to exit a Budokan match at any time, for example, if you decide you've selected the wrong art. But it costs you one match versus the current opponent.

Mike Tyson's Punch Out

By Nintendo
One Player

It's a right, a left, a right, and another left and he's flat on his back on the canvas! But don't get too confident – every fighter you face in this dynamite cart is likely to make you go another round. Mike Tyson's Punch Out is one of the most popular and biggest selling video games of all time! It's a title that really packs some punch.

Step into the ring as Little Mac, a 17-year-old fighter from the Bronx, ranked number three in the minor circuit. Your goal is to work your way up through the rankings so that you can challenge Mike Tyson, Kid Dynamite, in a dream fight!

READER'S TOP 20 CHOICE

But the road to the championship is long and hard. You'll have to work your way up through the minor, major, and world circuits by winning 14 bouts against some very tough opponents.

The rules of the World Video Boxing Association govern your bouts. Each match is three three-minute rounds long. Any boxer knocked down for a 10 count is Knocked Out (KO). If a boxer goes down three times, he'll find himself a Technical Knock Out (TKO). If both boxers make it to the end of the third round, the ref determines the winner.

Once you're in the ring you'll have to beat your opponent with smart fighting. Use left and right punches, as well as uppercuts to knock your opponent to the mat. Dodge your opponent's blows with some fancy footwork. Dazzle them with your brilliance and you'll be the World Video Game Champion before you know it! On the other hand, you might find yourself down for the count!

Hot ProTips

⭐ Watch your health meter! It takes energy to fight and you lose a little every time you throw a punch – whether you connect with your opponent or not! The key is that your opponent's health meter works the same way, and when you do connect with him he'll lose energy.

⭐ To begin each round in tip-top shape health meter-wise remember the following: never push your Start button while your coach is giving you advice. Hit Select as fast as you can while you listen to your coach's advice to get extra health when the round begins.

⭐ When either you or your opponent's health meter goes to zero, you'll find yourself flat on the canvas – a KO! Each time you go down in a bout it takes longer to get up, and you'll have to hit the buttons faster. But try not to get up until the count reaches nine. The longer you stay down, the more health you're rewarded with when you get up.

⭐ If you can connect with your opponent when your own stamina is very low, you'll get a small health boost. On the other hand, if your own health is low and you KO your opponent, he'll get a big health boost when he gets back on his feet.

⭐ The number of hearts you have equals the number of punches you have left. Every time you punch, whether you connect or not, you lose a heart. You'll also lose hearts when you get punched. If you get KO'd, you'll lose lots of hearts! When you run out of hearts you can't punch, and you have to rest. When this happens you've got big trouble because your opponent comes in for the kill and you've got no protection.

⭐ The number of stars you have equals the number of uppercuts you can throw. Your maximum is three, and you earn stars by punching

other boxers. Try using your uppercuts by first throwing a left and a
right, and then the uppercut.

⭐ Use your first two bouts, Glass Joe and Von Kaiser, to get the hang
of things. Practice your deadly left-right combinations, and throw a
few uppercuts to get the timing right. To knock Joe down with one
punch wait until the time reaches 40 seconds in the first round. Joe
will back up and make a face. As he comes forward (42-43 seconds), hit him in the stomach to send him straight to the mat. Use
a couple of regular punches to stun the Kaiser, and then blast him
with an uppercut.

⭐ Don Flamenco's famous for his deadly uppercut known as the Flamenco punch. He usually follows this up with a killer right hook.
Try dodging to the left when Don throws his uppercut, and then hitting him with a left-right-left-right flurry until he falls to the mat.
When he gets up he'll throw an uppercut. Hit him in the stomach
and you'll score a star! Repeat this until he goes down. In the first
match Don's second trip to the canvas is usually his last.

⭐ Piston Honda is quick on the draw, but he always lets you know just
what he's going to do by moving his eyebrows up and down! When
he does this dodge his jab, and try to throw a quick punch to his
head or he'll blast you with three jabs. Watch for Piston's little
dance. When he's finished he'll always throw an uppercut. Dodge
the uppercut and throw your own at the same time for a KO.

⭐ King Hippo is stronger than your previous opponent and he lets fly
with his cutting Guillotine Punch. When he bends his arms and
opens his mouth make your move and punch him in the face. His
pants will fall down! While he's trying to retrieve them punch him
in his weak spot – his stomach!

⭐ His first time to the mat will KO him.

⭐ The Great Tiger comes at you with a series of jabs right after his
ruby shines. When he ducks to the left, hit low and to the left.
When he ducks to the right, hit low and to the right. Each time you
do this you'll get a star. The Tiger has a Magic Punch that he sometimes uses at the end of the first round and always begins the second round with it. You can tell when he's about to throw this punch
because he'll take a step backwards first. Immediately get ready to
block. If you can block five of his punches in a row, he'll be
stunned. Now you can blast him with an uppercut.

☆ Bald Bull runs at you with a ferocious Bull Charge. You can't really dodge him too well, but you can fend him off by punching him in the stomach with your left during the third of his three hops. Bald Bull moves his hands quickly up and down right before he tries to blast you with his hook. Try punching him in the face with your left after he tries to blast you with his right uppercut. The second time you face Bald Bull, the only way to defeat him is to land an uppercut.

☆ Soda Popinski is pretty quick for a big guy. When he starts to shuffle his feet he's about to throw a flurry of punches. Dodge or block his punches, and then try to hit him with a series of rights to his face – you can land four to six blows if you're quick.

☆ Mr. Sandman tries to put you to sleep for good by moving his hands up and down quickly, pausing for a second, and then launching into his Razor Uppercut – a series of four rapid-fire uppercuts. Beat the Sandman by dodging and then trying to punch him in the face. Then go for a series of body blows to knock him to the mat.

☆ Super Macho Man is your toughest bout next to Tyson. When he comes after you try dodging left and then go for it with a series of jabs to his face. Watch out for his deadly Super Spin punch. After he throws an uppercut try to smash him with two quick jabs to the face for a star.

☆ Your toughest bout is the championship fight with Mike Tyson, Kid Dynamite. During the beginning of the fight Tyson throws nothing but deadly right and left uppercuts. Dodge left and then hit him with a few quick jabs to the face. You can reduce his meter by half if you can avoid his Dynamite Punch for the first minute and a half of the bout. During the second half of round one Tyson throws right and left hooks. Watch his eyes. If he winks with one eye, he's about to throw a straight punch. If he winks with both eyes, he's going to throw a flurry of straight punches. When he winks dodge to the left and go for two quick jabs to the head. Tyson begins round two with a storm of deadly body blows. Try to block or duck before you lose all of your hearts. Next, he's back to right or left hooks, so watch the eyes again. Eventually he'll pause for a moment and then throw a couple of uppercuts. Dodge, and then try to get up to six hits to the head. Watch for Tyson's other eye trick – he'll open both of them wide. Jump in and give him a quick body blow and then watch out for the four jabs he'll throw at you. Once you learn to recognize all of Tyson's patterns, you can go the distance with him and maybe even achieve the unthinkable – a KO!

Don Flamenco
   First Fight - 005 737 5423
   Second Fight - 647 993 3534

Major/Minor Title Holder
   777 807 3454

Piston Honda
   Second Fight - 667 833 7533

Super Macho Man
   237 210 7938

Mike Tyson
   007-373-5963

Play Another World Circuit – type in
   135 792 4680
and then hold down Select, and Buttons A and B simultaneously.

Get a Busy Signal On Your Game! Type in the Nintendo phone number for your password entry
   800 422 2602

By Tecmo
One or Two Players (simultaneous)

If you're a connoisseur of such skills as the Pile Driver, the Shoulder Throw, the Flying Knee Drop, the Metal Post Slam, and the ever-popular Scorpion Deathlock, have we got a game for you! To sample these and other vintage wrestling maneuvers you'll journey no further than a ringside seat in front of your nearest Nintendo. Plug in this cart and you'll find yourself in the Tecmo Coliseum attending the Tecmo World Wrestling extravaganza. Pro-wrestlers from around the world are competing for the Tecmo World Wrestling Crown.

Did we say ringside? Ooops! We meant inside of the ring! Yes, you're battling to win the coveted Tecmo World Wrestling Belt right along with the rest of them. And the rest of them include the likes of British Star (aka Rex Beat) from Britain, weighing in at 286 lbs, best known for moves like the Power Bomb and the Death Drop. Altogether 10 top notch wrestlers compete in the championship. Pick the wrestler you'd like to be and then battle for the belt against each of the other nine.

When your match begins you'll find you've got all of the moves of the pros. You can run, climb to the top of the ropes, climb outside of the ring, pick up your opponent, throw them over the ropes, pin them, and escape from a pin yourself.

So, you're a star! You've succeeded in pinning one wrestler. Well, don't get too revved up because you've got eight more to go. If you really want to wear that Tecmo Championship Belt you'll have to put your nose to the grind...er, that is, the mat and do some heavy duty wrestling.

Hot ProTips

⭐ Before each match begins you'll have the opportunity to "beef up" and do some training. This is your chance to strengthen your power meter for the bout ahead.

⭐ Each match is seven minutes long. You've got to pin your opponent before the time is up or the match is a draw. You'll lose the match if your opponent pins you. You can also get disqualified if you're caught on top of the ropes for a count of five or if you're out of the ring for a count of 20.

⭐ A good way to nail your opponent is to get him out of the ring, stay near the ropes, and just before you reach the 20-second limit jump back into the ring. Your opponent might get caught out of the ring and be disqualified.

⭐ Each of the wrestlers can make some mighty moves like the Body Slam or the Flying Knee Drop, but each wrestler also has specialty moves that most of the other wrestlers can't perform. This means that each wrestler has some special skills that make him unique. It actually gets even more complicated because some of the moves can only be done inside or outside of the ring, or when a wrestler has a certain amount of power. Check your manual for all the details!

⭐ Know your opponent and use your knowledge strategically. Don't use your opponent's super move against him and vice versa, try to use your super move against your opponent as often as possible – especially if it's a move your opponent can't do!

⭐ If your opponent has you cornered, run and jump off of the ropes by quickly pushing the appropriate direction on the controller two times.

⭐ Check out Tecmo World Wrestling's sound test by simultaneously holding diagonally Up and Left, Buttons A and B, and Select.

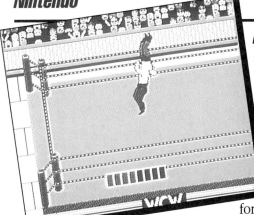

By FCI
One or Two Players (simultaneous)

You come out of your corner stalking your opponent warily around the ring. With a lunge you throw your speciality move, the "Flying Body Press." One! Two! Three! Pin your opponent for the count!

World Championship Wrestling introduces you to the rough and tumble National Wrestling Association by enabling you to be one of the 12 most popular NWA wrestlers. You'll recognize such greats as Road Warrior "Hawk" (whose favorite moves include the Brain Buster and the Boston Crab).

You have four game types to choose from. One Player Vs. the Computer mode pits you against each of the 11 other computer opponents twice before you finally face the WCW master. WCW also has One Player Tag Team vs. the Computer and Two Player Tag Team Vs. Tag Team modes.

Each wrestler has eight favorite moves and specialty moves – including such memorable body crunchers as the Cobra Twist, Boston Crab, Back Drop, and the infamous Pile Driver.

Your wrestler can also Run, climb onto the corner posts to execute such moves as the Diving Body Press and Diving Knee Drop, Fall on your opponent, and Drag your opponent by the feet. Even better, your moves aren't confined to the inside of the ring! Launch your attacks from on top of the ropes, climb outside of the ring to grab deadly weapons, or best of all, toss your opponent right out of the ring!

Altogether there's enough wrestling action here to keep even the biggest heavyweights hustling.

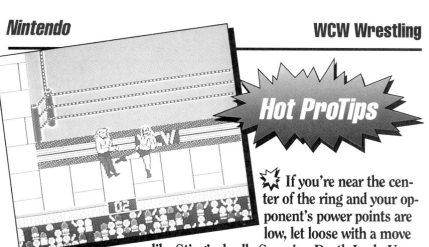

If you're near the center of the ring and your opponent's power points are low, let loose with a move like Sting's deadly Scorpion Death Lock. Use Button A to max up your power meter and you can do some serious damage to your opponent.

You can dominate the bout with kicking. There are three kicking actions you can use to defeat your opponents. First, try standing and kicking. If that doesn't work, try kicking and then moving forward and kicking. If this fails, try kicking and then moving backwards and kicking. Remember it takes a little timing and practice to master these moves.

There are different paths to victory. Get a Fall Count of three or drive your opponent's power bar to zero so they Give Up. If you use lots of special moves with maximum power, your opponent gets tired and gives up. You can also trick your foe into a Penalty Count of five or keep tossing him out of the ring until he's out of the match for good.

Here's a quick way to get a win: First, throw your opponent out of the ring. Next, wait until 12 to 14 seconds have gone by and perform a Favorite Move. Finally, wait until the 16-second mark and heave your opponent into the stands. If you do this correctly, you should win by an Out of Ring count.

To have a chance at victory against the WCW Master, you must use the Running Move well.

For an extra advantage use a controller with Turbo. Your super-powered kicks will send your opponent to the mat in no time.

Try all of your favorite moves with your favorite players and the following passwords:

Sting
Won 3 fights: BXDR NBQ5 19DQ
Won 6 fights: -XDY YBZH Y9DK
Won 9 fights: QXD- ØBØD L9DQ

Lex Luger
Won 3 fights: DXH5 NBD5 R9DK
Won 6 fights: LXHT YB67 N9DM

Rick Flair
Won 3 fights: DX7X NBT5 R9DV
Won 6 fights: BX7Z YB07 R9D1

Mike Rotunda
Won 3 fights: DXT9 NB15 R9DW
Won 6 fights: BXTH YB/7 R9DV

Kevin Sullivan
Won 3 fights: DXRZ NBY5 R9D5
Won 6 fights: BXRT YB6H R9D2

Rick Steiner
Won 3 fights: DXNH NB-9 R9D1
Won 6 fights: BXND YB4H R9D5

Ricky Steamboat
Won 3 fights: DX1T NBV5 R9DL
Won 6 fights: YX11 YB37 R9DD

Road Warrior Hawk
Won 3 fights: DXBR NBQ5 R9DG
Won 6 fights: BXB1 YB37 R9DD

Road Warrior Animal
Won 3 fights: DXYD NBK5 R9D6
Won 6 fights: BXYB YB57 R9DY
Won 11 fights: -XY- GBG1 R9DQ
Won 20 fights: N5Y1 1BP7 RZNT

Steve Williams
Won 3 fights: DXLN NBM5 R9D4
Won 6 fights: BXLY YB7H R9DV

Eddie Gilbert
Won 3 fights: DXJ1 NBW9 R9D5
Won 6 fights: BXJL YBTH R9DK

Michael Hayes
Won 3 fights: DXØB NB89 R9D7
Won 6 fights: BXØJ YBDH R9DW
Won 9 fights: JXØG ØBGD R9DV

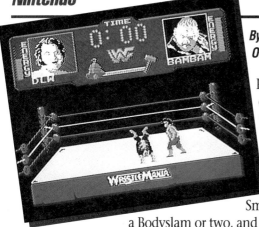

By Acclaim
One or Two Players (simultaneous)

In a bad mood? Have we got a cure for you! How you'd like to climb into the ring, take on the persona of Hulk Hogan, Andre the Giant, or even Bam Bam Bigelow, and throw a few Uppercut Smashes, a couple of Headbutts, a Bodyslam or two, and maybe even a Flying Elbow Smash for kicks? Well, get ready to go 'cause Acclaim's gathered all of the biggies from the WWF and put them into one jam-packed big-time wrestling cartridge – Wrestlemania!

Whatever your style of wrestling, it's here. Choose from several different ways to play including Tournament action where you pick the wrestler of your choice and then battle the other five in timed matches. If you've got two to six players you can go for ultimate tournament action! The wrestler with the most wins at the end of the Tournament is the champ and gets to wear the coveted solid-gold WWF Championship Belt!

READER'S TOP 20 CHOICE

The wrestlers that make up the Wrestlemania crew are some of the biggest names in the WWF – Ted "Million Dollar Man" DiBiase, Bam Bam Bigelow, Honky Tonk Man, Randy "Macho Man" Savage, Andre the Giant, and Hulk Hogan. Each wrestler has his own special strengths and abilities, based on his real-life skills. For example, Bam Bam Bigelow does his famous running Cartwheels, Andre the Giant has a mean Big Boot Kick, and Hulk Hogan's Turnbuckle move is a deadly Flying Leg Smash.

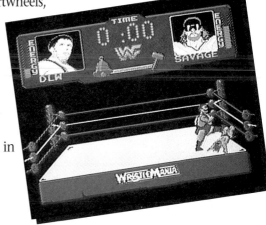

So you're in a bad mood? Well, like we said, climb into the ring with Wrestlemania and you'll be feeling no pain in no time at all!

Hot ProTips

⭐ There isn't any one wrestler who is particularly stronger than the others. Each has his own special moves and is well-rounded. Mastering each of the button combinations for an individual wrestler's up to eight different moves is a little tricky. Try picking one wrestler that you like best, and then practicing a lot with him to memorize all of his different moves. If you switch to different wrestlers, you'll find you get confused!

⭐ While you're in the ring keep an eye on your Energy Meter – and your opponent's. You won't be able to pull off some moves unless you've got more energy than your opponent. And if you've got zero energy, you're in trouble – you'll find yourself flat on your back on the mat in no time at all. You can also keep an eye on your Color Gauge. This measures how mad you are and the madder you get the more powerful you are! Watch for your individual Special Energizers (i.e. Macho Man's is a pair of shades, and Honky Tonk Man's is a guitar). Grab the Energizer to max up your Energy for a special move.

⭐ Four of the wrestler's have Turnbuckle moves that are performed from the ring post. To defend against these moves simply stay away from the center of the ring when your opponent is running back and forth. He can only jump so far from the post and he'll miss you if you're out of the center and towards the back of the ring.

⭐ The moves you can make on your opponent when your back is to him are often very effective because they catch him off guard.

⭐ If your energy meter is low, your best strategy is to avoid contact with your opponent by staying away from him! While you're running around your energy comes back.

If your opponent's energy is low, try to keep between him and his Energizer. You don't want him getting any stronger when you've got him on the ropes.

 If your opponent pins you, hit the Up button as rapidly as possible to get your energy back and get to your feet. You might avoid the count!

 It's a little tricky to get the hang of pinning your opponent. Once you've got them down you have to be standing just to the side of them, and then hit Up or Down and either A or B depending on your wrestler. This takes practice but becomes automatic once you get used to it.

 When you're fighting an opponent and his music comes on, you can bring your own music back by simply hitting Pause and then un-pausing.

CHAPTER 9
Sidewalk Shreddin'

By Mindscape
One Player

What's a "720"? Rowdy wheelheads know it's an aggro aerial move! But for you non-skateboarders it's a gravity-defying mid-air 720 degree double spin – get it?

You got it! 720° showcases the 720 and other rad moves. The object is to skate straight through a grid-like system of city streets to four skating events – the Downhill, the Slalom, the Jump, and the Ramp – where skillful skating scores more points and wins you medals so you can advance through the levels.

As you tear through town, you can zoom off ramps and leap over ponds, grass patches, and other obstacles for points. You also dodge motorcycle maniacs, crazy cars, obnoxious joggers, and frisbee-tossing freaks. Naturally, you pull 720's as often as you can to earn points. While you're at it grab some cash to buy hot skating equipment – helmets, boards, pads, and shoes – and tickets to the events.

There's no mystery to any of the contests. The Downhill is a wild ramp-hopping ride against time. In the Slalom you scoot through flag gates to beat the clock. In the Jump, you, uhhh, jump a monster ramp and go airborne. The Ramp is an excellent half-pipe where you pull slides, handplants, and handstands. Rack up enough points and you move onto another level where everything's the same (except for the colors), but you get less time and tickets cost more.

There's little change of scenery here, but the skating's fast, fluid, and fun. Only hardcore skaters need apply.

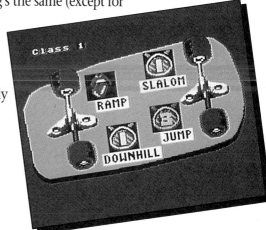

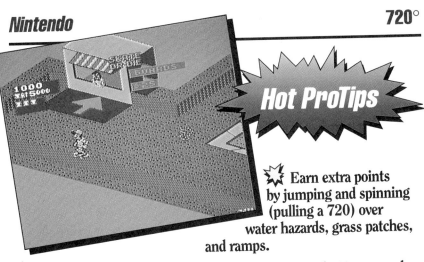

Hot ProTips

☆ Earn extra points by jumping and spinning (pulling a 720) over water hazards, grass patches, and ramps.

☆ The timer at the Main Park counts down 40 seconds. Ten seconds later, the Killer Bees arrive. Each time you enter an event you reset the Main Park timer.

☆ Bees always swarm from the right side of the screen, so skate away from that direction when "Skate or Die" flashes onscreen.

☆ If the bees are on your tail, hit a map symbol. It takes several seconds for the bees to find you when you exit the map screen.

☆ To save precious seconds when you leave the map screen, decide where you want to go and hold down the directional pad in that direction before you exit the screen. You instantly take off that way when you reappear in the Main Park. That can really save you when the bees are on your tail.

☆ Entering an event is the only way to completely escape the bees.

☆ If there's time on the timer when you find an event entrance, build up points by doing 720's there until the timer runs down. Enter the event just before the bees arrive.

☆ During the Slalom, the Jump, and the Downhill jump and spin whenever you can to score extra points.

☆ At the end of the Downhill ramps, angled arrows indicate the direction that the next ramp slopes. It takes practice but if you can anticipate the end of the ramp and pull a 720 onto the next ramp at a slight angle to the direction of the arrow, you can score extra points and dramatically speed up your run.

☆ The Ramp is the toughest event to master. Once you learn a move, keep repeating it. You can still earn a medal (even the gold) that way.

☆ On the Slalom it's better to go through a gate in the wrong direction than to skip it altogether.

☆ To reach peak performance take time to upgrade as much equipment as you can at each level. The board and the shoes are the bare minimum you need.

☆ You can bounce off the fence, but try not to jump into it. Even if you complete the jump, you won't score any points. Also, there is a spot where you hop over the fence. Then, all you can do is wait for the bees to arrive.

By Ultra
One to Eight Players

If you think all sports take place in squeaky-clean stadiums or on manicured grass, you've got a lot to learn. Here's lesson No.1 – Skate or Die. S or D is a classic NES skateboarding cart. Don't let Rodney Recloose and his gang of skate fiends fool you. This is a sports game in adventure clothing that cops a king-size thrill for skateboarding maniacs.

Skate or Die's got all of the rad moves. You tackle five events – the Downhill Race, the Jam, the High Jump, the Joust, and the Freestyle – all of which are take-offs on actual skateboarding events and require unique moves. Hone your riding skills in Practice Mode, and then take on Rodney's gang in the Compete All Street mode. Beat the bad boys and etch your name onto the Trophy Screen.

The game is great for group play. Up to eight people can skate at once (taking turns, of course). Also, there's a handicapping feature called Goofy Foot. The onscreen perspective doesn't change, but right becomes left and up becomes down. It's more of a challenge than it sounds, and it's a great equalizer when good skaters play the uninitiated.

If you're any kind of skateboarding enthusiast, this is the cart for you. The Downhill, the Freestyle, the Jam, and the Joust will really grab you. The High Jump's a bit monotonous, but four out of five ain't bad. Hardcore thrashers always brag about being able to skate anything. Alright, Skate or Die!

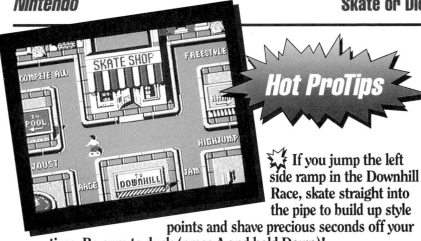

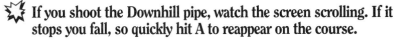
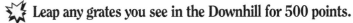
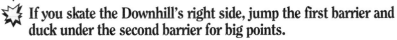
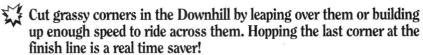

If you jump the left side ramp in the Downhill Race, skate straight into the pipe to build up style points and shave precious seconds off your time. Be sure to duck (press A and hold Down)!

If you shoot the Downhill pipe, watch the screen scrolling. If it stops you fall, so quickly hit A to reappear on the course.

Leap any grates you see in the Downhill for 500 points.

If you skate the Downhill's right side, jump the first barrier and duck under the second barrier for big points.

Cut grassy corners in the Downhill by leaping over them or building up enough speed to ride across them. Hopping the last corner at the finish line is a real time saver!

Looking for another Downhill challenge? Try hopping across the pond.

Just after the first wire fence in the Jam, scoot over to the far left. There's a time-saving opening through the building you can't see. Ride a line to the left of the can. Snatch the can if you can.

You can kick and punch your opponent in the Jam, but another good wipe-out is to get slightly ahead of him and then cut into his path.

In the Jam, jump over the black and yellow speed bumps or they slow you down.

In the High Jump press Button A at the top of your jump to add a few extra inches.

Got a controller with Turbo? Use it in the High Jump.

✦ On defense during the Joust, watch your oponent's position and take a circular evasive pattern. Your opponent has to chase you over a lot of territory that way.

✦ On offense during the Joust, take a tight figure eight pattern to intercept your opponent's path. Stay alert when the stick changes hands, sometimes you can score a quick hit. But turnabout is fair play!

✦ In the Freestyle, the longer you hold a Hand Plant the more points you score. But hold it too long and you wipe out.

✦ Something unclear in the instructions: When you do Ollies in the Freestyle, press Button A at least twice in the Pump Zone, press the directional pad forward (in relation to the direction you're skating) to jump, THEN press the pad in the opposite direction to stop the turn in mid-air for a solid landing.

✦ Put the cursor on the trophy in the opening screen to see the high scores. Just for kicks, check out other on-screen items, too.

By LJN
One or Two Players

Feeling a little bored? How about some board action! It's a really radical cure for what ails you. Get ready to kick it out with a crazy bunch of skate and surf groupies. From jumping the cracks and jammin' the ramps to riding the waves and rippin' the surf, T & C Surf Design is one sure cure for board-om.

Hey, it's two, two, two games in one! Sometimes known as Wood and Water Rage, this title gives you the choice of either climbing onto your favorite skateboard to try and navigate down the boardwalk or paddling out to ride the waves on a surfboard.

Skateboarding, or the Street Skate Session as it's called in the game, lets you become either Joe Cool or Tiki Man. Once your Skate Session starts you've got to zip down the boardwalk, avoiding all kinds of wild obstacles while you try to reach the end in a certain amount of time. Score points by collecting special items and making some radical moves.

For some alternate board action head to the Big Wave Encounter. Here you get to be either Thrilla Gorilla or Kool Kat. Your goal is to ride the waves all the way to the beach. Along the way you'll score points by shredding, making turns, riding inside of the Pipeline, and picking up floating bananas. You'll have to avoid some gnarly hazards including jumping fish and flying seagulls.

To make it through both the Street Skate Session and the Big Wave Encounter intact, you'll have to remember what it takes to win – smooth moves, high scores, and always, always keep your cool!

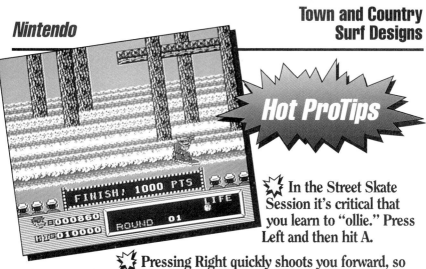

Hot ProTips

⭐ In the Street Skate Session it's critical that you learn to "ollie." Press Left and then hit A.

⭐ Pressing Right quickly shoots you forward, so be prepared!

⭐ To make a jump off the ramps and clear the crevasse, first press B rapidly to build up momentum. Now, make sure at least the tip of your board touches the lip and then pull an Ollie (press Left and then A).

⭐ Grab all the red Bonus Coins. The third coin in possession is worth 1200 points; every one after that is 2400 points.

⭐ The faster you skate, the more Life Symbols you earn up to eight total. When you earn the eighth Symbol, you freeze the clock for a Time Bonus ride.

⭐ For a super-fast ride and a tough challenge, use a controller with turbo.

⭐ You can Ollie to snatch coins that appear "above" you onscreen.

⭐ Riding the tall (4-beam) guardrail is an easy 1000 points (not 500 as stated in the manual). Riding the regular rails isn't worth any points, but it's a move that can get you out of tight spots. But remember, once you hop a rail you can't jump off.

⭐ In the Big Wave Encounter, you want to ride the wave as long as you can. At the start, press Right and A to surf across the wave and away from the Pipeline. Now, you have room to pull cool turns for extra points.

To stretch out your ride, press Up and B to quickly head towards the top of the wave, and then press Right and A to zoom a little further across the wave.

 If you only have one or two Life Symbols left, forget style points for turns and try to land on the beach to advance to the next round.

 If you're caught in the Pipeline, keep your weight forward by pressing A and then hitting Right. You can score points and surf out of the tube, although you'll wipe out eventually.

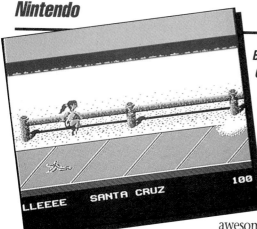

By Milton Bradley
One to Eight Players

Hey guys and gals – are you ready for sun, surf, sand, and rad action? Well, dudes, it's time for California games. That's right, check out how the folks on the West Coast compete in some of the most awesome sports around.

Choose game options that let you compete in all or some of the six events, or just chill out with one event in particular. Like, go for it yourself, or like, wow, you can make the scene with up to seven of your buds.

Cruise the state of California, and hang out in some of the coolest spots for these six totally tubular events. Hooray for Hollywood where you'll spin and fly with awesome moves on your skateboard in the Half Pipe event. Head for the City by the Bay, San Francisco, to show your slick tricks and fancy footwork with the Foot Bag. Next, like, hit the beach for Surfing and Rollerskating. Things get pretty gnarly in the desert, where you'll battle it out in a BMX Bike Racing blitz. Like, wind things up at Yosemite for some fresh action with the Flying Disk.

If you go way aggro, you can max out your points in each event. You might even get to try to stuff a first, second, or third place trophy into your fanny pack. Snag enough high scores in each of the different events and you're the California Games Champ, with your very own radical high scores on the High Score Screen.

Like, would you miss the gnarly action of this totally rad California scene? No way, dude! It's too totally tubular to be true!

⭐ Rack up big points in the Half Pipe with some slick tricks and excellent timing. Max up your speed to make your stunts, but not too fast or you'll wipe out. For Aerial Turns, turn immediately once you take off from the ramp. Always kick turn opposite the direction you are facing. Don't let go of your hand plants on the top of the ramp until your body has spun past the apex of your rotation.

⭐ Sure you get the most points by pulling some slick Foot Bag moves like the Double Arch, Dizzy Dean, or the Doda. But an easy way to rack up a lot of points quickly is to kick the bag off the field and catch it when it comes back in!

⭐ Your catches are more important than your throws in the Flying Disk event. You get more points for fancy catches than you do for throwing the disk far.

⭐ Play it fast and loose in the Surfing event. If your ride isn't aggro enough, you won't score well. For the biggest points catch some air off the crest of the wave. Watch out for the wipeout!

⭐ Like, if surfing makes you dizzy, try flipping your controller upside down! Now you're making your moves in the same direction as the surfer!

⭐ BMX takes stamina and skill. Jumps are easy as long as you land flat on both wheels. 360's on flat surfaces are an easy way to rack up points. Go for backward and forward flips only off of high jumps!

⭐ When you're Roller Skating avoid obstacles and you'll score points, but you'll score higher if you jump over the obstacles, and even more if you jump and spin! Speed doesn't count as much as staying on your feet. Once you've got the hang of the moves you can go for faster speed.

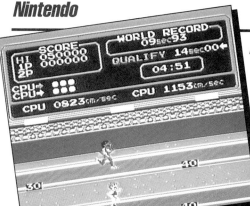

By Konami
One or Two Players (simultaneous)

Strap on your spikes and head for the track to rip into one of the sports games that started it all – Konami's Track and Field. This title pits you against some fierce competition in all of your favorite track events – the 100-Meter Dash, the Long Jump, the 100-Meter Hurdles, the Javelin Throw, Skeet Shooting, the Triple Jump, Archery, and the High Jump.

Style your track meet any way you like it. Play from novice to advanced levels against the computer (and your own scores), or go head-to-head versus a buddy. You'll really feel the pressure as you try to beat your opponent's scores and come up with the highest point total to prove you're the best.

In each individual event you can work to beat your own record or aim for the World Record displayed in the upper right-hand corner of the screen. But before you go for the top spot, you've got to match or beat the qualifying time, distance, or score or you can't even advance to the next event. You get three tries to qualify in each event. Don't foul too many times or you'll find yourself disqualified with nothing left to do but kick the ground and shake your fists. Depending on the event there are different ways to foul. Jump the gun in the 100-Meter Dash or the 110-Meter Hurdles and you'll foul. In the Javelin Throw, the Long Jump, and the Triple Jump you must avoid running beyond the limit marker. In each event you're allowed three fouls before you're disqualified.

READER'S TOP 20 CHOICE

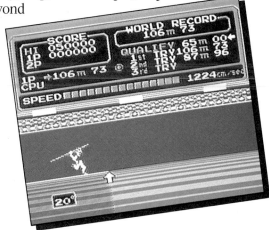

Don't miss this one – you're just a hop, skip, and "long-jump" away from a field-full of fun.

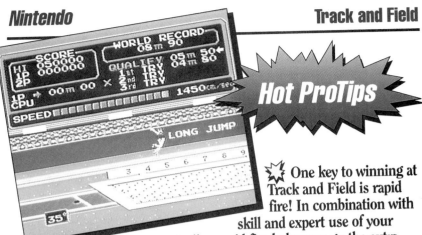

Hot ProTips

⭐ One key to winning at Track and Field is rapid fire! In combination with skill and expert use of your game controller, rapid fire helps you go the extra distance that makes you the champ!

⭐ Play it conservative in your first try at any event. Once you've qualified you can let it all hang out, take some chances, and go for that World's Record!

⭐ With rapid fire and a good start the 100-Meter Dash is a snap!

⭐ Rapid fire helps you pick up the speed you need to turn in a World's Record in the Long Jump. Try keeping your jump angle in the 35-50 degree range.

⭐ The key in the 100-Meter Hurdles is timing and getting into a pattern. It's a good idea not to charge into the first hurdle too fast because if you miss that one you'll tend to be off all the rest of the distance. Hit the first hurdle and you can get into a rhythm, pick up speed, and blow right by your opponent.

⭐ Sprint to the line with Rapid Fire and toss your Javelin at a 30-45 degree angle for an easy World's Record!

⭐ Yipes! Skeet Shooting is one of the toughest events! You can try using one gun or the other to avoid jam ups, and keep an eye out for the blue clay target that appears when you've blasted several white targets in a row. Peg this blue skeet – it's worth big points, and it's the only way to get a World's Record.

⭐ Use rapid fire to run to the line at top speed and then take your hop, skip, and jump at an angle of 40-50 degrees for a great Triple Jump.

⭐ In the Archery event you'll have to take wind speed and shot angle into account while you try to hit a moving target! Try releasing your arrow just as the center of the target passes the bottom edge or the large target at the top of the screen or the upper right-hand corner of the scoreboard on the bottom right of the screen. Keep your shot angle as close to five degrees as possible. Be sure to fire an arrow into the funny figure who occasionally appears after you hit a bull's eye. Spearing this little guy gives you big bonus points!

 Watch for one of these three strange competitors – the Jocular Pig, a UFO, or the Mole. They can mean 3,000 bonus points for you!

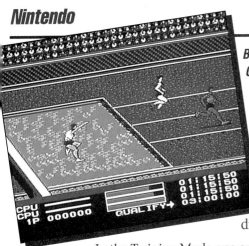

By Konami
One or Two Players (simultaneous)

This sequel to Track and Field is definitely a GamePro pick and one of the hottest sports games of all time! In Konami's classic Track and Field II you'll compete in more than 13 different events in three different modes.

In the Training Mode one or two players can practice their skills and warm up in the 12 individual events. Learn to excel in training and you'll do well in the tough competition of the Olympic Mode. As the team of your choice (ten teams including the USA, France, and the USSR) you'll fly to the Olympic Games in a special Konami jet. Once you've taken in the opening ceremonies you'll have to demonstrate all of your strength, stamina, and skill in many grueling days of competition. If you're good enough to qualify, you might even make it to the last three days of the competition – the Finals! Who knows, maybe you'll even wind up with a nice collection of gold medals! The competition events in the Training and Olympic Modes include Fencing, Triple Jump, Freestyle Swimming, High Dive, Clay Pigeon Shooting, Hammer Throw, Taekwondo, Pole Vault, Archery, Hurdles, and Horizontal Bar. And if you're really good, you might even get to try out some unusual events like Hang Gliding.

READER'S TOP 20 CHOICE

For some variety try the Versus Mode and match up against a friend in Arm Wrestling, Fencing, or Taekwondo. It's the thrill of victory, the agony of defeat, and, well, mostly the agony of defeat! But hey, everybody can't be an Olympic star!

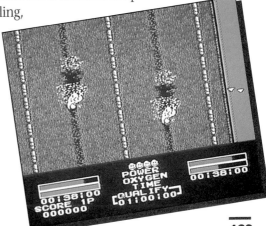

Hot ProTips

⭐ Use a controller with rapid-fire mode! You may think your trigger finger is super fast, but just as in Track and Field, you'll have a much better chance of qualifying and racking up higher scores (and save a lot of wear and tear on your fingers) if you use the rapid-fire mode.

⭐ Read the detailed instructions in the manual!! This game requires many specialized moves too difficult to figure out on your own.

⭐ In Fencing the safest attack move is the low thrust. Lunge forward while pushing A and Down, and you might catch your opponent off guard. When you're on the defense, parry your opponent's jabs and quickly take the offensive with the low thrust or the more risky high thrust (A and Up) while your opponent is off guard.

⭐ In the Triple Jump success is just a hop, skip, and jump away with a rapid fire controller! Use rapid fire to build up speed before you make your hop, avoid stepping over the foul line, use B to get a 45-degree angle on your hop, and qualifying is a snap.

⭐ Rapid fire is key in the Swimming events – but don't forget to breathe! If you want the computer swimmer in a one-player game to swim butterfly instead of freestyle, try pressing Down on Control Pad II before you dive off of the blocks.

⭐ In the High Dive you'll need to mix up your dives by doing as many different moves as possible. To straighten out before you hit the water stop tapping the buttons about two body lengths above the surface of the water.

⭐ Clay Pigeons fly out of the grey area of the bunker nearest to you. If you can't blast them right as they're thrown (when they're closest to you and easy to hit), try to pause a fraction of a second, line up the pigeons in your sights, and then peg them as they're falling.

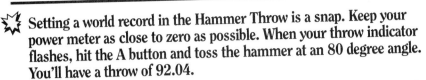

Setting a world record in the Hammer Throw is a snap. Keep your power meter as close to zero as possible. When your throw indicator flashes, hit the A button and toss the hammer at an 80 degree angle. You'll have a throw of 92.04.

In Taekwondo, charge your opponent and clobber him with repeated roundhouse kicks to his mid-section by hitting Down and Button B.

The key to the Pole Vault is a combination of lightning speed in your approach (rapid fire) and a great pole plant. To avoid fouling, aim to plant your pole in the center of the square at the base of the bar.

During Kayak training, familiarize yourself with the order of the gates so you are prepared ahead of time to move forwards or backwards. To increase your speed stay near the center of the course, away from the river banks.

In Archery remember that the farther away from the target you are the more you have to correct for the effects of the wind. To correct for crosswind move your bow to the left or right. Angle the bow higher and max up your power for longer distances. At 70 Meters try angling your bow up between 05 and 06. For 90 meters angle the bow at 09.

The Hurdles feature an unusual twist – water hazards! The Olympic Record in this event is tough to beat! Blast out of the blocks as soon as the gun goes off. Use rapid fire to max your speed and build up the momentum to fly over the water hazards. Time your leap over the hurdle carefully, and hold B down longer to make sure you clear the larger water hazards.

The Horizontal Bar requires a tricky juggle of power and finesse. Blast away at the A button to max your power while you perform a dazzling gymnastics display. You'll score higher if you keep performing different moves as quickly as possible. Impress the judges with your speed, agility, and variety! They get bored easily!

Continued on Page 172

Last Day of the Olympics Passwords:

2M1SPZJWS	Soviet Union
54HLPHJNI	United States
5ZHDPZJ2S	France
DAVYYHJTS	Germany
YAWWWHJ4S	Great Britain
3QWIWJJIS	Korea
EECYWHJGS	China
WAIYWHJLI	Canada
3QYGPJJFL	Kenya
LKWTWHJPS	Japan

By Epyx/Milton Bradley
One to Eight Players

Experience the thrill of victory and the agony of defeat as you travel across the world to compete in eight different international events. In World Games you become an athlete representing one of six countries.

As the games begin, decide if you'd like to practice an individual event, compete in some events, compete in all events, or just check out the world records. Since each of the eight events has an international flavor, the game options also include a travelogue feature that enables you to exercise your mind as well as your body! Each travelogue tells you a little bit of the history behind each sport in the competition and why it's associated with a particular country. For example, you probably didn't know that the Caber Toss, where athletes heave a tree trunk the size of a telephone pole, originated in ancient Scotland.

The events themselves range from the more familiar Weight Lifting and Slalom Skiing to the more exotic Barrel Jumping, Cliff Diving, Log Rolling, Bull Riding, Caber Toss, and Sumo Wrestling.

Although you can play World Games with only one player, it's much more fun with two or more players. In each event computer judges score the athletes' performances and award medals to the top three competitors. If you play on your own, you always get the gold medal in each event unless you fault. However, you can always play to break some World Records so you can etch your name on to the World Records screen. Play with friends, though, and you can enjoy the thrill of winning medals in individual events as well as beating out your opponents to fly home as the all-around Grand Champion!

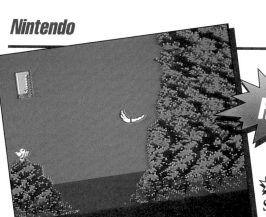

Hot ProTips

⭐ In Weight Lifting the Snatch is relatively easy, requiring you to just press Down, Up, Down, and Up. The Clean and Jerk, however, is a lot more complicated. You need to press Down, Up, Down, Up, Down, and Up, and you need to do it at just the right time or you won't make the lift. Practice both lifts at easy weights until you've got the pattern and timing down, and then advance to the World Record levels.

⭐ The trick with Barrel Jumping is to build up your speed, keep it going, and successfully time your take off. If you're concentrating on your speed too much, it's easy to miss your take off, and smash into the barrels. If you're concentrating on your take off, you tend to let up on your speed just at the crucial moment. Coordinate both of them and you'll clear 15 barrels easy.

⭐ Cliff Divers should first practice at lower levels. This gives you a gradual feel for how much you need to arch to clear the rocks as well as when to straighten out your dive. The longer you arch the farther away from the rocks you land – and the lower you score! So, fine tune your dives to just clear the rocks and go for it!

⭐ Balance is obviously the key to winning the Log Rolling contest. To stay on your log you've got to learn how to adjust your lumberjack's leg speeds in conjunction with the balance bar at the bottom of the screen. This one just takes practice. Hit the A button quickly to reverse the log direction and hopefully knock your opponent off the log.

⭐ Just as in many of the other events, the key in the Caber Toss is getting the hang of moving your player's legs in a smooth enough rhythm to build up his speed quickly. You've got to increase the tempo gradually and smoothly. Wailing away at the Left, Right controls doesn't work! Once you've got your speed up, hit A two times to plant your feet and toss the Caber. Again, this just takes a little practice.

 There are 12 different moves to master in Sumo Wrestling. It may not be elegant, but one strategy that often works for us is just to randomly hit your controller and the A button. You make a lot of moves quickly and your opponent is often totally baffled – next thing he knows, he's on his backside out of the ring!

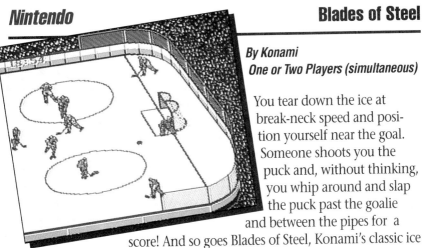

By Konami
One or Two Players (simultaneous)

You tear down the ice at break-neck speed and position yourself near the goal. Someone shoots you the puck and, without thinking, you whip around and slap the puck past the goalie and between the pipes for a score! And so goes Blades of Steel, Konami's classic ice hockey cart for the NES.

One or Two Players face off on the ice in Blades of Steel. The One Player Mode offers a choice between Exhibition and Tournament play. In Exhibition play you pick your team and a computer team to match up against in a one-game competition. In Tournament play you become one of eight Canadian or American computer teams (New York, Chicago, Los Angeles, Montreal, Toronto, Edmonton, Vancouver, and Minnesota) and play the other seven teams in tournament action.

READER'S TOP 20 CHOICE

This cart gives you all of the glamour and all of the action of real ice hockey. Each game begins with an opening face off and includes authentic hockey play right down to the brawls and altercations between opposing team members. Game play on the ice is fast and furious as you can control each of your team members, including your goalie. Mount an aggressive offensive attack, do some hard checking to get a defensive advantage, and even provoke a fight. Great graphics and fabulous gameplay have made this title a legend in its own time. It's up to you to get ready to use your edge to put your opponents on ice!

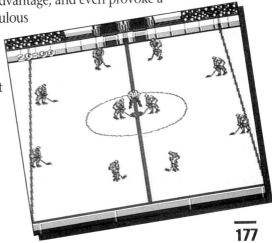

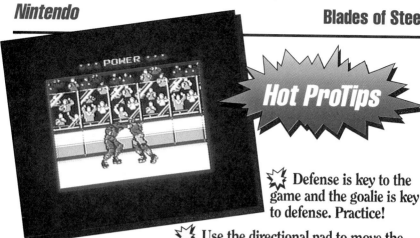

 Defense is key to the game and the goalie is key to defense. Practice!

Use the directional pad to move the goalie out of the net to cut off shooting angles, but watch out! Shots can bounce off the goalie and into the net!

Each of the eight teams are different. Here's the rundown:

New York: Well balanced.
Chicago: Great speed, but no standout shooter.
Los Angeles: Fairly fast and aggressive – heavy duty checking!
Montreal: Strong with speed, and a break-away offense. Aggressive.
Toronto: Great offense, but weak defense.
Edmonton: Break-away offense and good speed.
Vancouver: Great shooting!
Minnesota: Good skating and precision shooting.

You can usually win the face-off if you press A rapidly just before the ref yells, "Face-off!"

It's poor sportsmanship, but starting a fight is a good strategy in this cart. If you win, the other side temporarily loses a man. Keep body checking the player with the puck until he can't take it anymore.

Body check by bumping into the man with the puck. Hit him three times in a row and you knock him down.

When you get into a fight, start punching immediately by rapidly pressing Button B. Otherwise your man gets knocked down and the refs drag him off of the ice. If you're quick on the draw, you should almost always win a fight against the computer.

If penalties leave you short-handed and your opponent is swarming all over your defense, try to steal the puck and quickly press A to shoot it down to the other end of the ice. This buys you time to re-group your defense and possibly spring a man from the penalty box.

 On offense, go for the powerplay! Don't waste time on too many long shots. Rush the net.

By Hot-B
One Player

If you're tired of running, dribbling, kicking, and other more mundane sports activities, then get your hooks into Hot-B's unusual Black Bass Fishing cart. Now you can recreate that most ancient of struggles – Man versus Fish.

Designed with input from real fishing enthusiasts, Black Bass Fishing simulates the ups and downs of fishing very realistically – including the fact that it takes a long time to catch a fish! Although you'll hook up with vicious pike, rowdy rainbow trout, and brawny brown trout, your real quarry is that elusive monster of the marshlands – the largemouth bass.

The object of the game is to win the fishing tournament by catching the most bass. You won't catch a fish with every cast, and you'll have to work your way up through three classes and 200 individual rankings to reach the top of the heap.

Fish at one of four different lakes. At each lake you move your boat around searching for the best fishing spots near submerged tree stumps, tall marshgrass, old pier pilings, and deepwater points. You'll have to assess the weather conditions and time of day to select the best locations. You'll also have to pick your lure.

Sight-in your cast, and when the lure hits the water, start the retrieve. Shadowy fish shapes chase your lure, but you won't know what kind of fish they are until one hits! If a fish chomps on the lure, reel it in – but not too fast or you'll lose it! With a little patience, skill, and luck you might even land the big one! Or you can tell some great fish stories about the one that got away!

☆ Lake Amada is where you'll catch bass most frequently, but they're on the small side. Japan Lake is full of mid-sized and small bass. Lake More and San Lake are where the super-large lunkers live.

☆ The Spinner is the best all around bass lure, but when all else fails, use the worm! Let it sink to the bottom then press the directional pad Right or Left. Occasionally, hit the A button to make the worm dance along the lake bottom.

☆ Sometimes lure color is the key to increasing your chances of getting a bite. Red is the best color for evening fishing. Silver is excellent for clear days.

☆ You can get pretty good at casting your lure into specific spots, but cast too far left or right and you'll lose your lucky lure off-screen. In general, cast straight down the middle of the screen and use the direction key to maneuver the lure into the right spot.

☆ The action of the lure is what attracts the fish. Press Left then Right on the directional controller to make your lure wiggle, but when the fish starts to follow it, press Up to make it move away from the fish. He'll think his lunch is trying to run away and almost always goes for it!

☆ If you've got a little fish on the line and you don't want to lose time by messing with it, just press Select to unhook the fish without reeling it all the way in.

☆ When you're reeling in your line, don't go too fast or you'll lose the fish – along with your line and lure! Ringing bells mean you're putting too much pressure on the line. Remember, be patient!

Class B –

> TSVWDEDØDIBPUYCG

Class A –

> HRVQSE14EZH2M1XS

By Romstar
One to Four Players

Sure, bowling started with the caveman, but to Americans it has its own special mystique! And this cart captures it to a B. So settle back for a little bowling, couch-potato style.

Based on the rules and regs of real bowling, Championship Bowling pits one to four players against one another in ten regulation frames. Scoring is based on scratch bowling. You win by having the highest score based on pin count. A perfect score is 300.

As the game begins you select the number of players and pick from five different lanes to bowl on. After you've selected your alley, you get to choose which bowler you'd like to be. Each of the four has different abilities – such as the ability to hook, left or right-handedness, and strength. When the preliminaries are over and the pins are lined up it's bowl, bowl, bowl gently down the lane. Use Button A to set the Control (whether your shot goes straight down the lane or hooks) and the Power (how hard you bowl the ball) of your ball as it rolls down the alley. Your score is based on how many pins you take out! You get two tries on each of your turns and if you knock down all ten pins in one turn it is, of course, a strike.

If you score more than a few strikes, you never know – a couple of cheerleaders might even show up to give you an extra "rah-rah" or two. Bowling? You bet!

⭐ Each of the bowlers is different. The left-handed and right-handed bowlers are mirror images of each other, except that the right-handed bowler seems to have a slightly better hook, although with the right control the left-handed bowler can also hook well. The strong bowler and the woman bowler have similar skills, except that the strong bowler can roll the heavier ball with more success.

⭐ Step number one to success in Championship Bowling is mastering the use of the Control bar. Hit Button A once to get the bar swinging and again to lock it into place. If the dot is locked at 12:00 (straight up), your shot will basically go straight down the alley. How far the dot ends up to the left or right (i.e. 10:00 or 2:00) determines how much your ball will hook.

⭐ Step number two to success in Championship Bowling is figuring out how the Power Meter works with the Control Meter. If you put a hook on your shot but use lots of power, your shot won't actually hook much. The lower your power, the more your shot hooks. Practice using different combinations to get a feel for getting the kind of shots you want.

⭐ Although the lanes are supposedly different we didn't find that we had to bowl any differently. There's more variation among the different bowlers than among the lanes.

⭐ If you're a bowler, try using basically the same strategies you'd use in real bowling in this video version of the sport. You can aim using either the pins (Pin Bowling), the spots on the lane (Spot Bowling), or the lines on the chart to the side of the lane (Line Bowling). We were at our most accurate when we used our bowler's head to line ourselves up with the spots on the lane.

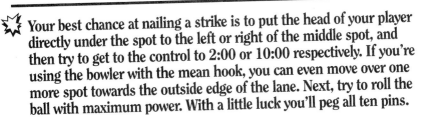 Your best chance at nailing a strike is to put the head of your player directly under the spot to the left or right of the middle spot, and then try to get to the control to 2:00 or 10:00 respectively. If you're using the bowler with the mean hook, you can even move over one more spot towards the outside edge of the lane. Next, try to roll the ball with maximum power. With a little luck you'll peg all ten pins.

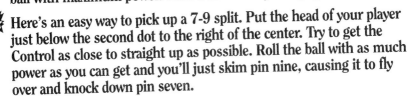 Here's an easy way to pick up a 7-9 split. Put the head of your player just below the second dot to the right of the center. Try to get the Control as close to straight up as possible. Roll the ball with as much power as you can get and you'll just skim pin nine, causing it to fly over and knock down pin seven.

By Parker Brothers
One or Two Players

You've heard of skiing, you've heard of surfing, but have you heard of snowboarding?? This hot new sport you play in the cold is one of the fastest growing pastimes in the United States, Europe, and Japan. Try to imagine a combination of downhill surfing, skateboarding, and sailboarding, and you'll begin to get an idea of what it's all about.

The snowboard itself looks like a cross between a ski and a surfboard. Once you climb aboard you'll compete in five different events with a total of 18 different levels of competition. The Downhill is flat out fast-as-you-can skiing down a snowy slope. In the Slalom event you zig zag your way through a series of gates. The Half-Pipe is just like skate boarding! It requires balance and some fancy stunts to do well here. Careen down a hillside packed with Moguls (bumps in the snow), and then finally, the Backwoods Event. Here you'll have to pull off death-defying stunts that include leaping over a waterfall or a crevice.

To make it successfully through the competition, master all of the snowboard moves. You'll have to learn to turn, duck, jump, and stunt. Stunts are for fun (hot doggin') and also, in some cases, for survival! Try such nifty moves as the Toe Grab, Mid-Air 360, Hand-Plant, and Mule-Kick!

With the right combination of skill, fancy moves, and just plain guts you might find yourself king of the snowboard mountain. If you lose your nerve, just remember, when the going gets tough, the tough go shreddin'!

Hot ProTips

⚡ Don't attempt any stunts on the Downhill portion of any course. Usually you have just enough time to complete the course with a straight run. Any hot doggin' could cause you to run out of time.

⚡ You can successfully leap the truck located at the "backwood" portion of Widowrun by tucking before you hit the ski jump. Be sure not to hit any buttons or stand up during your jump.

⚡ When you crash or fail to complete a portion of a course, check the upper right-hand corner of the screen to see what maneuver you should have made.

⚡ Survive big jumps during a slalom by doing a Mule-Kick stunt (Button A and Left on the directional key) then regain your balance and turn towards the next set of gates.

⚡ The key to surviving the half-pipe is to perform your jump, then turn and head back down into the half-pipe again. Be sure not to jump up over the edge of the pipe when you perform your maneuver.

⚡ In the half-pipe, stunts must be executed immediately when they are requested, or you will not have enough time to complete the required number. When you are requested to perform a "jump", hit the 'A' button without using the directional controller or else you will wipe out.

⚡ Survive the mogul run by doing regular jumps over the larger groups of moguls. Do not attempt any stunts or you'll run out of time.

⚡ Listen for the waterfalls up ahead when you're on certain backwoods trails. You'll have to perform a double jump (once onto the patch of ice in the middle of the stream, then off the ice and back onto the snow) to clear the falls.

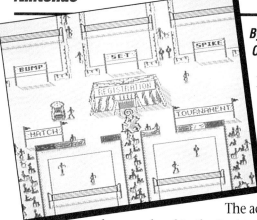

By Ultra
One to Four Players (simultaneous)

If you're ready for sun, sand, surf, and volleyball, here's your chance to strip down to your shorts, show your moves, and end up on top of the heap, or as they say "King of the Beach."

The action gets movin' and groovin' when you head to the Registration Tent at the beach to pick your style of competition for up to four players. Game play is two on two. The pros include the likes of Sinjin Smith and Randy Stoklos, each with his own unique style.

Before you make the tournament scene you can cruise to the Practice Courts to practice your Bumps, Sets, and Spikes. When you're ready for the agony of defeat head back to the Reg Tent and then hit the beach. If you choose Match Play, you and up to three friends can battle it out in a one-game match to 15 points or the best two-out-of-three 12-point games.

Tournament action gets hot and sandy on five different beaches worldwide. It's you and one other player going against the Kings of the Beach. To get to each of the five different stages (beaches) in the tournament, you'll have to win three consecutive 15-point games.

The volleyball action itself is true to the game with the same rules as real volleyball. In addition to the more run-of-the-mill moves, like the set, spike, and block, you've got some heavy-duty moves that will blow your opponents out of the sand.

Like we said, it's sun, surf, sand, and volleyball. So grab your shades and get ready to catch some rays. If you're willing to sweat a little you might end up as King of the Beach. Can you dig it?

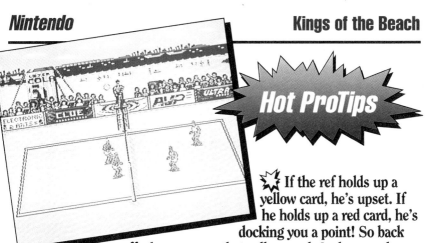

Hot ProTips

⭐ If the ref holds up a yellow card, he's upset. If he holds up a red card, he's docking you a point! So back off when you see that yellow card. And remember, you've got to disagree with the ref's call before the score appears.

⭐ Use the shadow to position yourself to hit the ball – stand right on it. It takes practice to get the timing down.

⭐ Timing is one of the keys to a successful outing in Kings of the Beach. You can't spike the ball every time. The computer opponent will catch on to anything you do if you do it too many times in a row. Mix up your shots and the areas you aim for, and when the time is right, spike it into the computer team's faces!

⭐ It is important to have your player positioned where he does the most good. Think of two-man volleyball as a doubles tennis match. If your partner is playing the net on the left side, position your player in the back court, slightly to the right. If you position your player properly, there will be fewer places for the computer to aim for.

⭐ The Jump Serve is extremely effective during the early rounds of the tournament. Press a button to toss the ball, and then press A to jump and smash the ball.

⭐ Prepare for the ricochet. Never assume spiking a ball is going to get you an automatic kill. In later rounds your opponent will almost always be ready to block your spike attempt. Your partner probably won't be in position to get the rebound, so it's up to you to get the ricochet.

Stage 2 – San Diego, California

Side Out

Stage 3 – Waikiki Beach, Hawaii

Gekko

Stage 4 – Copacabana Beach, Rio De Janeiro

Topflite

Stage 5 – The Great White Beach, Australia

Sundevil

By CSG Imagesoft
One or Two Players (simultaneous)

The stalwart U.S. Dodgeball Players have teamed up to challenge their opponents from around the globe for the title of World Cup Champions. Their ultimate goal is to wallop the undefeated Soviet team. Take command of your buffed U.S. team and work your way up to victory!

Super Dodge Ball is vigorous sport consisting of two teams with six players on each side of the rectangular court, three players in and three out. The object is to clobber your opponents and deplete their energy by hurling the hard ball at them using various different throwing techniques and as much speed as possible.

World Cup Play pits the U.S. team against eight other countries in the quest for the World Cup. In Versus play you can challenge your friend or play with your friend against the computer. For a little practice try a Bean Ball match.

READER'S TOP 20 CHOICE

When the action starts your team tries to wing the ball at your opponent's team members, and they hit you. You can pass the ball to a teammate, catch it, or throw it. When a player gets hit enough times hard enough, he is simply whisked away (courtesy of an angel) and play continues. When you've eliminated your opponent's team you win.

You may or may not have played dodge ball in the school yard, but either way you'll quickly get hooked. Although seemingly simplistic, Super Dodge Ball has all of the makings for good old fashioned sports competition. Nab this one and take home the World Cup, dodge ball style.

Hot ProTips

Besides the basic moves each international team in Super Dodge Ball also possesses a unique skill, such as excellent throwing power, agility, ball breaking, catching technique, energy, fancy throwing techniques, and damage capacity. Overall some teams are more powerful than others, especially the tough Soviet team whose players all have extremely high energy levels.

Most players have a specially timed "power shot" or two hidden up their sleeves. There are 13 different "power shots" that can unexpectedly slam an unsuspecting opponent or simply psyche him out. For example, the Psycho breaks up into many balls, and the Warp disappears in the air, only to reappear right in front of your opponent.

Catch your opponents offguard! Have one of your inner-court players run the ball towards the centerline. Jump, and use Button A along with the directional controller to throw a fast pass to a teammate on the outer court. Your teammate will automatically jump up and deflect the ball at an opponent.

Plan your Team USA inner court carefully. Try Sam. Only players on the innner court can use the special "power" shots and Sam's "Blaster" is devastating! Often it can damage more than one opponent at a time. John is well-suited for the inner court. He can take the most punishment before he loses energy. Steve or Bill make good choices for your last inner court player. Steve has excellent power shots. Bill is the most agile member on Team USA. He can survive the longest by ducking and jumping.

As long as the ball stays in your possession, you can continuously throw the ball at an opponent who is down and rack up damage.

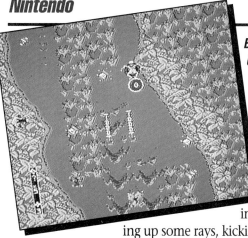

By Tengen
One or Two Players

If you're game to try a little sports action with a twist, then get out your pump, inflate your favorite inner tube, and let's go toobin'! Toobin' is when you float down your favorite river in an inner tube, just relaxing, soaking up some rays, kicking back...well, maybe on a regular river, but snooze off in this game and you'll find yourself sinking fast! Get ready for some wild ride!

Become either Bif, or in a two-player game, Bif and Jet taking turns on the river competing against each other. In the special one-player mode, use both controllers to control Bif. One player can make Bif toss cans while the other steers Bif down the river.

You start off with a few cans, a few inner tube patches, a pair of shades, and of course, your trusty tube. As you cruise down the river you'll see treasure chests, floating cans and six packs, gates, beach balls, patches, and letters. Grab these things cause you're gonna' need them!

Each river is also packed with obstacles – some annoying and some downright dangerous. You'll have to dodge everything from giant yellow dinosaurs to cacti to diving penguins.

Your goal is to become a Class 9 toober, and navigate your way down all 49 rivers – from the murky, sludgy waters of a modern city, to the strange purple water of a Martian Canal. But it'll take some mean toobin' to get that far!

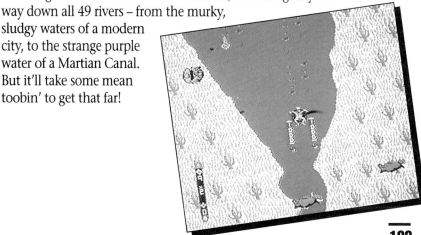

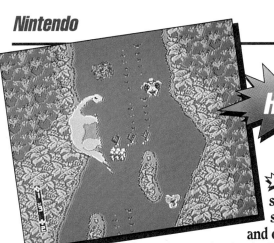

Hot ProTips

⭐ You can temporarily stun your enemies who shoot guns, axes, spears, and other nasty things at you from the riverbanks, by hitting them with cans. Then you can fly by without any danger.

⭐ Make sure and grab the floating six-pack when you see it. You'll get more than the maximum of nine cans, and you'll need them all! Once you've got the six-pack you can heave cans at all of the obstacles without worrying about your supply!

⭐ Snag the spinning beach ball and you'll be able to fling your cans farther and faster.

⭐ You gotta' go through the gates to keep your score multiplier maxed up. Miss a gate and your multiplier is back to zero. Ease through the gates without hitting the sides for maximum points.

⭐ Don't go flying down the river as fast as you can! That's a sure way to end up with a popped inner tube. Navigate down carefully and slowly (with an occasional exciting ride on the white water) and remember it's more important to conserve patches than to pick up every item you see.

⭐ Grab three letters and you'll get a new toob and three extra patches. Grab all seven letters in the word Toobin' and you'll get a choice of extra lives or big bonus points.

⭐ Jam down enough rivers successfully and you get to celebrate at a wild party on the beach.

Nintendo   Arch Rivals

By Acclaim

If you enjoy basketball of the "basket-brawl" variety, check out this new title. This is slam-dunkin', full-court basketball where anything can and does happen. One or two players can choose from six different rough-and-tumble basketball stars. Play in teams as you attempt to do whatever it takes – from stealing the ball to punching out your opponent – to score the most points during the game. To get into this game you've gotta' want to beat the other guy – literally.

Battle Royale   TurboGrafx-16

By NEC

What do you think a game entitled "Battle Royale" is about? Well, if you guessed a family squabble between Chuck and Di, you lose. This cart showcases BRAWL (Battle Royale of America Wrestling League) and pits up to five players at once against each other in big-time wrestling action. When the game begins you're a manager, and your first task is to race to the dressing room door of the wrestler of your choice. From there on out it's wild and crazy wrasslin' with the likes of Spitfire Spike and The Meat-Eater. Grrrr....

Genesis   Hard Drivin'

By Tengen

If you hang out at the arcades, this title needs no further explanation! But those of you unfamiliar with Hard Drivin' can get ready to climb behind the wheel of a high perfor-mance super stunt car for the ride of your life! The thrills that await you include vertical loops, high-speed races, high-flying jumps, and a 360° loop. You can even jump across an open drawbridge. A change of pace from the other racing titles, this one promises to be as big a smash at home as it is in the arcades.

By Sega of America

After James Buster Douglas knocked out Mike Tyson he headed over to Sega of America and scored big once again! He joins the Sega team by putting his name to, what else, a boxing title! The cart features arcade-style (in fact, it looks just like Final Blow) boxing action. You go head-to-head with other boxers from a side view. The graphics are great (really big sprites) and the sound is good. You'll almost feel like you're in the ring, but fortunately you won't feel the pain when you get KO'd!

Joe Montana Football

Genesis

By Sega of America

San Francisco 49'ers super quarterback Joe Montana has been drafted by Sega to star in a football title being developed for several different systems, the arcades, and, of course, the Genesis. The game promises 16 different teams each with their own playbooks, 18 offensive and 16 defensive plays per team, realistic play-action, individual player characteristics, and much, much more, including the "Joe Cam" (which shows digitized pictures of Joe's reactions to his great plays!). This one looks like it's headed to the Super Bowl of football carts.

Nintendo

Matchbox Racers

By Matchbox

Sure, everybody remembers those great little Matchbox cars, but did you know that Matchbox has brought them to life? That's right, now you can race Matchbox racers, Mega-Speed boats, or even Demolition Derby cars in this new title for the NES. The game features an isometric 3-D track. You'll have to watch out for all kinds of obstacles, including tunnels, two-way jumps, and even attacks from other racers. To survive use your turbo speed, supergrip, hydrofoil, and special weapons. Matchbox fans everywhere are gonna love this one!

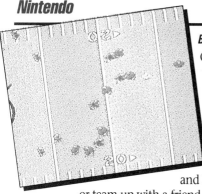

By Accolade

Get ready for gridiron action with lots of wide-open – that is, "big play" – offense. You get a horizontally- and vertically-scrolling overhead perspective, and a wide range of offensive and defensive options, including the ability to change plays in mid-stream if the defense is shutting you down. Each of your players is rated for Dexterity, Agility, and Body. Play against the computer or a friend, or team up with a friend for real bone-jarring action. This is a great title for those who want a video sports challenge without a thick manual to master.

Mondu's Fight Palace   Genesis

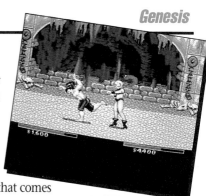

By Activision

For wrestling action the likes of which we guarantee you've never seen before, journey far into the future – 2550 to be exact. When you step into the Fight Palace you'll find Mondu-the-Fat, undefeated champion and host at the Palace, is challenging all comers to hand-to-hand combat, or tentacle-to-hand combat, or, well, you get the idea. Mondu himself battles with a giant tongue that comes out of his stomach (computer gamers will recognize this title as Tongue of the Fatman). Like we said, it's wrestling like you've never seen it before!

Genesis   Super Monaco GP

By Sega of America

Super Monaco GP brings it on home with the arcade-style racing action that made this title a smash coin-op. Look for all of the same great graphic features that gave the arcade hit that heart-stopping sense of action. Your car features great handling – you shift gears and monitor speed and other variables – and you're also low to the ground for a realistic race-car perspective. You get a great racer, tough Grand Prix tracks, and big prizes. What more could you want? You'll be on the fast track to success in no time at all.

Super Volleyball

By NEC

When you think of volleyball do you think of tans, beaches, and sun? Well, Super Volleyball is a change of pace! This is World Tournament volleyball action. It takes place in a stadium packed with fanatic fans. Compete as one of eight international teams in a tournament series, or design your own team and play in a one-game series. The players are rated on key volleyball skills – spike, set, return, serve, and block. The volleyball here is serious - it'll take more than a tan to earn you the tournament cup.

T.V. Sports Basketball

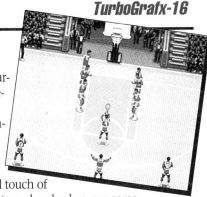

By Cinemaware/NEC

T.V. Sports Basketball is the next in Cinemaware's series of T.V. Sports titles for the TurboGrafx-16. This card features full-court five-on-five basketball, just like you see on T.V. Look for players with different skill levels, individual team stats, digitized sound and music, and arcade-style action on offense and defense. On court you call the shots, and make them too! And just for that added touch of realism the game also includes T.V. broadcasters, cheerleaders, pre-game and post-game shows! Who needs T.V.?!

Ultimate Basketball

By American Sammy

Get ready for fast-paced hoops in this first in a series of Ultimate sports titles from American Sammy. The game features full-court five-on-five basketball with you as coach, player, and even bench warmer! Make the hot plays, score points, go for the slam, or a three -pointer. You can even substitute in fresh players from the bench. The game features lots of close-up full-screen animation and you can play against the computer or a friend, or team up with a friend against the computer. It's the ultimate in basketball!

By Jaleco

There's only one sport that features grabbing, punching, slamming, and hair-pulling all on wheels – Roller Derby! War On Wheels puts you right in the middle of a round-robin Roller Derby competition for the international championship! Once you've strapped on your skates and the whistle blows, it's anything goes! Do whatever it takes to crash past your opponents and score enough points to win your match and make it to the next round. Even the fans are just crazy enough to join in on the action!

World Trophy Soccer

By Arcadia

Here's another arcade translation of a top coin op title – World Trophy Soccer. If you enjoy soccer, or "football" as it's called in the rest of the world, then you should get a kick out of this cart. It's your chance to join the USA's World Cup and Olympic team for world class soccer action as you dribble, pass, tackle, and shoot your way to victory. Can you get a leg up on the international competition?

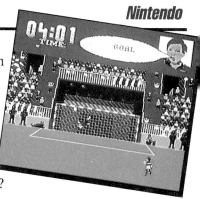

By Electronic Arts

Ho hum, another golf game. Stop!! This is Zany Golf which means nine of the most, well, unusual holes of golf you'll ever see. Picture miniature golf with a lot of imagination thrown in. This means holes with surprises like magical fairies who give you extra strokes or a jumping Hamburger Hole with squirting ketchup, or even a hole with a hole that moves! Sometimes you'll find that your ball may unexpectedly vanish or disappear in a burst of fireworks. It's unique, it's outrageous, it's, it's, ZANY!

Be Sure to Check Out This Other Great GamePro Hot Tips Book!

The best gets better—because there's also an Adventure Games version of the GamePro Hot Tips Book! *Over 120* of the best games are reviewed, with dazzling full color screen shots throughout—including *over 940* winning strategies, tons of tips, Secret Weapons And Tactics (S.W.A.T.), and valuable game-ending passwords! The Nintendo, Genesis, & TurboGrafx-16 systems are all covered—because they're the ones you've told us you want!

Nintendo ▼ Genesis ▼ TurboGrafx-16

Available Now at Stores Near You. Or, Order Directly From IDG Books With The Coupon Below.

HOT TIPS: ADVENTURE GAMES

ver 940 ew Tips, Tactics, ecret Passwords Strate Make Power ayer!

Inside: Money Saving Coupons!

120 edible

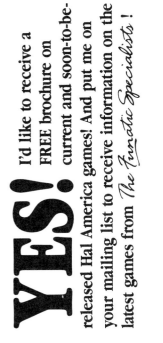